MOSQUITO

FIGHTER

SQUADRONS

IN FOCUS

RED
KITE

First published 2005 by
Red Kite
PO Box 223,
Walton on Thames
Surrey, KT12 3YQ

© 2005 Philip Birtles

Printed in England by
Cromwell Press.

ISBN 0-9546201-3-5

Designed by
Simon W Parry

Introduction

To fit into the format of this book it has been necessary to split the Mosquito units into two, starting with the Fighter based versions serving with the RAF. The Mosquito changed very little in overall configuration during its service, being produced in two basic versions – the Fighter and Bomber. The original Mosquito was designed as an unarmed bomber and indeed the type never carried defensive armament, but could certainly pack a significant punch when armed with fixed nose mounted machine guns and belly mounted 20mm cannons. The fighter/FB airframe had a flat bullet-proof windscreen, a "solid" nose housing four .303in machine guns with armour plating behind, and as four underfloor cannons blocked the original access, the crew entered from the side of the cockpit. The Mosquito T.Mk.III trainer was based on the fighter airframe.

The major development of the Mosquito was increasing the warload and range by fitting progressively more powerful Rolls-Royce Merlin engines. The structure was almost entirely of wood, utilising non-strategic materials and labour. It was operated by a crew of two and was faster than any other combat aircraft during World War II until the arrival of the jet powered fighters. On initial tests at Boscombe Down, the Mosquito prototype was found to be some 20mph faster than the Spitfire. and it was soon realised that the type would make an excellent long range fighter. With the approval of the Chief of the Air Staff, John Cunningham was invited by Geoffrey de Havilland to fly the Mosquito Prototype before any other service pilots. Having been operating Blenheims and Beaufighters fitted with early AI radar, John confirmed that the Mosquito would make an excellent night fighter. As a result, the third Mosquito, W4042 was completed as a night fighter, and it was flown out by Geoffrey de Havilland Jnr from fields adjacent to Salisbury Hall on 15 May 1941. The Mosquito night fighter was progressively developed with improved radars housed in nose mounted radomes, which replaced the .303in machine guns. However, the four cannons could pack a punch and were more than enough to down an enemy aircraft.

The Mosquito Fighter made a very useful intruder aircraft until replaced by the FB.VI which combined the punch of four .303in machine guns and four 20mm cannons with a bomb carrying capability, both internally and under the wings. The FB.VI was the most plentiful mark of Mosquito, but now few exist. In addition to intruding, the Mosquito FB.VI was used for precision bombing of selected targets in built up areas, and also as a light bomber and armed photo-reconnaissance aircraft. The later have been included in this account due to the common airframe. The Mosquito FB.VI was also adapted as a potent ship buster and anti U-boat aircraft with underwing mounted rocket projectiles (RP) and the Mk.XVIII had the original four cannons replaced by a powerful Molins 57mm cannon, which was particularly effective against U-boats.

Some of the units were camera shy due to the short duration of service, or remote location of the bases. Therefore generic photos have been used as illustrations in these cases, but if anyone can help illustrate Mosquitos of these units please contact the author, via the publisher.

Philip Birtles February 2005.

Bibliography

Bomber Squadrons of the RAF & their Aircraft, by Philip Moyes, published by Macdonald 1964

Coastal Support & Special Squadrons of the RAF & their Aircraft, by John Rawlings, published by Jane's 1982

de Havilland Aircraft, by A J Jackson, published by Putnam 1962

Fighter Squadrons of the RAF & their Aircraft, by John Rawlings, published by Macdonald 1969.

Mosquito – A Pictorial History of the DH.98, by Philip Birtles, published by Janes 1980.

Mosquito – The Illustrated History, by Philip Birtles, published by Sutton 1998.

RAF Flying Training & Support Units, by R Sturtivant, J Hamlin & J Halley, published by Air-Britain 1997.

Front Cover:
A Mosquito FB VI in 1944.

Inside front cover:
A classic view of a Mosquito NF II.

Previous Page:
A Mosquito FB VI, made by the Standard Motor Company, during an engine test.

Facing Page:
A Mosquito dispersal at Hunsdon.

CONTENTS

DEVELOPMENT

The Mosquito was originally developed as a high speed unarmed bomber. The prototype was designed and built in secrecy at the remote location of Salisbury Hall, some four miles from Hatfield. The design team was housed in the moated historic mansion with a hangar disguised as a barn built on the other side of the moat. Here the prototype W4050 was hand built in 1939 and 1940, before being moved by road to Hatfield for the maiden flight by Geoffrey de Havilland Jnr on 25 November 1940. The main reason for the secrecy was not so much to keep the work from the prying eyes of the Germans, but to avoid the project being cancelled by the British Government. de Havilland had started work on the prototype as a private venture while the Hatfield factory was busy producing Airspeed Oxfords and repairing battle damaged Hurricanes.

The Mosquito design team reasoned that what was required was an aircraft more cost effective than the currently planned four engine all metal heavy bombers with a crew of up to ten and bristling with a heavy defensive armament. The guns on the bombers were only capable of defending against hostile fighters, therefore if the guns and associated crew and armour plating were removed, the aircraft would go faster due to reduced weight and drag. It would no longer require four engines, reducing to two Merlins and operated by two crew – a pilot and navigator/bomb aimer. Why not make it from wood, a material with which de Havilland were familiar? Not only was it a non-strategic material using labour otherwise not employed on defence work, but it gave a smooth finish without rivets and was easy to repair in the field. Wood is more resilient than metal and in the event of a belly landing could often be back in the air in a short time. Later bomber versions of the Mosquito were able to carry a 4,000lb "Cookie" blast fragmentation bomb, which was a greater total load than the B-17 Flying Fortress. Mosquito bombers could fly to

Berlin twice a night and the loss rates were far less than with the heavy bombers.

Once the prototype had proved itself at the A&AEE at Boscombe Down, the Ministry of Aircraft Production placed an initial order for 50 Mosquitos, but were undecided on which role required the greatest priority, as there was also an urgent need for high speed photo reconnaissance and fighters. As a result the third airframe W4052 was completed as the first NF.II night fighter, in an enlarged hangar at Salisbury Hall.

The Mosquito Night Fighter was fitted with an early form of Airborne Interception (AI) radar with a double arrow head antenna in the centre of the four nose mounted 0.303in machine guns and whip aerials above and below each wing tip. The aircraft was guided on to the hostile target by ground based radars and, when located by the crew, the navigator guided the pilot to just behind and below the target to ensure it was identified as an enemy aircraft. The pilot then brought the Mosquito up behind the target and fired the combined machine guns and cannons to hopefully gain a success against another German raider roaming over Britain, bombing its cities.

With improved AI radar equipment the Mosquito night fighter became a major part of the night defence of Britain. The newer radars were housed under protective radomes which displaced the four nose mounted machine guns. The first of these was AI Mk.VII fitted to Mosquito DD715 in July 1942, and following successful trials 97 Mk.IIs were taken from the Leavesden production line and delivered to Marshalls of Cambridge for the fitting of radomes. After the fitting of the secret radar equipment at RRE Defford they were designated NF.Mk.XII entering service with No.85 Squadron in February 1943. The similar NF.Mk. XIII was developed from the FB.Mk.VI with the fuel in-

Above: **Early production Mosquito night fighters at Hatfield awaiting delivery to squadrons.**

Right: **The prototype FB.VI built at Hatfield. It was later destroyed in a crash landing at Boscombe Down after engine failure.**

Right: **Mosquito NF.XIX MM682 with the thimble nose radome. This aircraft was attached to the Fighter Interception Development Unit at Ford.**

Right: **The instrument panel of a Mk.VI showing the armour plate bulkhead on the starboard side.**

development of the basic FB.VI was the Mk.XVIII known as the Tsetse with the four 20mm cannons replaced by a single 6lb Molins cannon. The FB.VIs could carry eight 60lb rocket projectiles (RP), two 500lb bombs or two 100 gal (454 litre) drop fuel tanks under the wings. The Mk.XVIIIs were mainly used against U-boats in the Bay of Biscay, the 37mm shell being aimed at the base of the conning tower, punching a hole in the hull.

One special version of the fighter was produced to combat high flying Ju86 nuisance raiders in the summer of 1942. The initial conversion to the high altitude Mk.XV was from the pressure cabin bomber prototype MP469 powered by a pair of Merlin 61 engines and a surplus four machine gun nose, which had been removed from a fuselage when a radome was fitted. The weight was reduced by removing the armour plating and reducing fuel as well as many other detail changes and the first conversion was rolled out for engine runs only a week after the go-ahead. The first flight was on 14 September 1942 and an altitude of 43,500ft (13,259m) was reached. MP469 later had the nose mounted guns replaced by a radome and the guns were moved to a ventral gun pack below the bomb-bay. A further four B.Mk.IVs were also converted to NF.Mk.XVs to be used by No.85 Squadron at Hunsdon from April until August 1943 when the high level threat had gone away. These were the only Mosquito fighters to be fitted with a Vee-windscreen as they were converted from B.Mk.IVs.

Left: **The 20mm cannons are being cleaned and the 303 machine guns rearmed on this No.23 Squadron FB.VI in Italy.**

Below: **Armourers load explosive shells into the feeds for the 20mm cannons in a Mosquito FB.VI.**

creased from 547 to 716 gal (2,486 to 3,255 litres). With the availability of airborne radars from the USA, a new universal radome was produced to house both the British and American radars. The first to be fitted was DZ659 in January 1943 with American AI/SCR720 equipment to become the NF.Mk.XIX. A further 98 NF.IIs were taken from Leavesden for conversion at Cambridge to NF.Mk. XVII. In April 1944 the NF.Mk.30 was developed from the Mk.XIX with more powerful two-stage Merlin 72s. The final Mosquito night fighter for the RAF was the NF.Mk.36 powered by more powerful Merlin 113 engines and with improvements to the radar. The ultimate Mosquito night fighter was the NF.Mk.38 with even better radar and most of the production run from Hawarden was delivered to the Yugoslav Air Force.

Without the AI fitted, the Mosquito F.II was used as a fighter/intruder, flying over enemy territory and attacking targets of opportunity in the air and on the ground, having originally started as an escort fighter for bombers. This version was so successful that it was developed into the FB.Mk.VI which was not only armed with four .303in machine guns and four 20mm cannons, but also bombs in a reduced bomb bay and later under the wings. The first FB.Mk.VI was DZ434 making its maiden flight in June 1942, later becoming HJ662 and making an effective ground attack (and with underwing RP also an anti-shipping) aircraft. The FB.VI remained in production for the remainder of the war with more built than any other variant. With the benefit of the forward firing armament, FB.VIs took over the low level precision bombing role from the more vulnerable unarmed bombers. The only significant

4 SQUADRON

Code Letters:

UP & NC

Usage:
Mosquito FB.VI

Aug 1945 – Jul 1950

Bases:
Volkel 8 – 9.45
Gilze-Rijen 9 – 11.45
Gutersloh 11.45 – 11.47
Wahn 11.47 – 9.49
Celle 9.49 – 7.50

Above: **Believed to have been operated by No.4 Squadron, Mosquito FB.VI HJ756 was destined to be flown to a MU for salvage and scrapping. However, after departure from Gatwick, engine problems made a return a wise decision. The aircraft undershot on the approach, skidded across the airfield sideways and demolished a hut. It would have been occupied, but the residents were outside at the NAAFI wagon.**

Above: **A line up of No.4 Squadron Mosquito FB.VIs at Celle in Germany in the autumn of 1949, with air and ground crews.**

Service history: No.4 Squadron was disbanded at Celle on 31 August 1945, but on the same day No.605 Squadron at Volkel was renumbered No.4 Squadron equipped with Mosquito FB.VIs. On 10 July 1950 the squadron moved to Wunstorf to convert to Vampires.

Usage:
Mosquito FB.VI
Oct 1948 - Aug 1950

Bases:

Wahn 10.48 – 9.49
Celle 9.49 – 9.50

Left: **The ubiquitous FB.VI soldiered on in occupied Germany long after the war.**

Service history: On 4 October 1948 No.107(B) Squadron was renumbered No.11(B) Squadron at Wahn in Germany in the bomber role. A move was made to Celle in September 1949, and then to Wunstorf for conversion to another de Havilland product, the Vampire jet fighter.

Below: **Mosquito FB.VI LR356 fitted with underwing bombs being made ready for a test flight from Hatfield in March 1944. This aircraft is similar to the FB.VIs operated by No.11 Squadron in occupied Germany after the war.**

Usage:
Mosquito FB.VI
Sept 1943 - Oct 1947

Bases:

Sculthorpe 9.43 – 12.43
Hunsdon 12.43 – 4.44
Gravesend 4.44 – 6.44
Thorney Island 6.44 – 2.45
France 2.45 – 4.45
Brussels 4.45 – 11.45
Gutersloh 8.46 – 11.47

Above: **A No.21 Squadron Mosquito FB.VI KR356 on a *Noball* operation – the destruction of V-1 launch sites, photographed from a No.109 Squadron Mosquito.**

Below: **Mosquito FB.VI PZ306 YH-Y of No.21 Squadron flying over France on 18 March 1945. Note the different styles of the upper wing roundels worn by these two aircraft.**

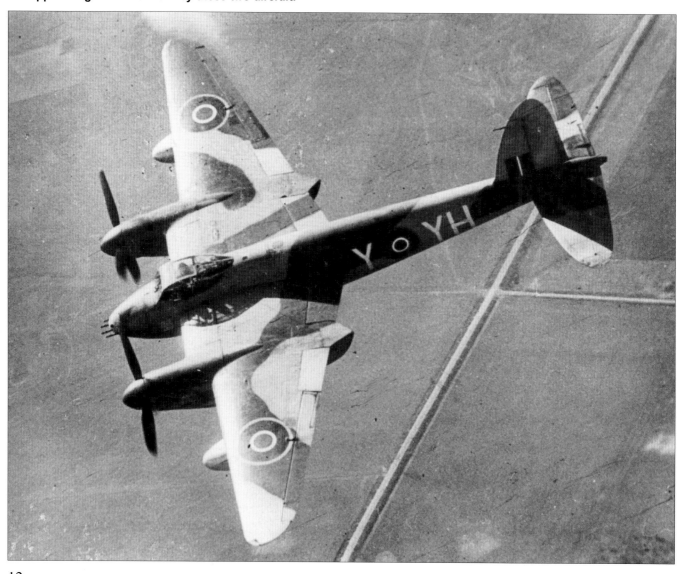

22
SQUADRON

Usage:
Mosquito FB.VI
May 1946 - Aug 1946

Base:

*Seletar, Singapore
5.46 – 8.46*

Above: **No.22 Squadron operated Mosquito FB.VIs similar to this. The squadron reformed as a fighter squadron at Seletar 1 May 1946 by renumbering No.89 Squadron, but disbanded on 15 August the same year.**

Below: **A flight of No.21 Squadron Mosquito FB.VIs over France on 18 March 1945.**

Service history: No.21 Squadron converted from Venturas in September 1943 to Mosquito fighter bombers which were used on night bombing and a number of daylight precision attacks including the *Gestapo* headquarters at Aarhus in Denmark on 31 October 1944 and Copenhagen on 21 March 1945. One of 21's Mosquitos, LR385:D made a total of 104 operational sorties starting with a V-weapon site on 6 February 1944, and finishing with a railway attack on 29/30 November 1944. After the war, the squadron operated courier services between Nuremberg and Blackbushe during the war-crime trials.

SQUADRON
Code Letters:
YP

Usage:
Mosquito F.II
Jan 1942 – Aug 1943
Mosquito FB.VI
May 1943 – September 1945
Mosquito NF.30
Aug 1945 – Feb 1947
Mosquito NF.36
Feb 1947 – May 1952

Bases:

Ford 10.40 – 8.42
Manston 8.42
Bradwell Bay 8.42
Manston 8.42 – 9.42
Bradwell Bay 9.42 – 12.42
Luqa, Malta 12.42 – 9.43
Italy 9.43 – 5.44
Little Snoring 6.44 – 9.45
Wittering 9.46 – 2.47
Coltishall 2.47 – 11.49
Church Fenton 11.49 – 9.50
Coltishall 9.50 – 1956.

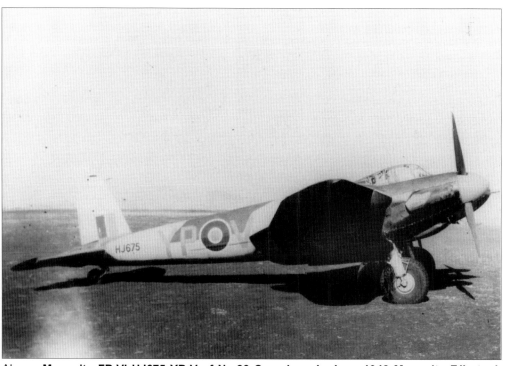

Above: **Mosquito FB.VI HJ675 YP-V of No.23 Squadron.** In June 1942 Mosquito F.IIs took over the long range intruder role from Bostons and Havocs with No.23 Squadron, moving to Malta at the end of the year to support the planned invasion of Sicily and Italy. By mid 1943 most of the targets were out of range, changing to daylight operations until returning to Britain in April.

Below: **No.23 Squadron was the unit tasked with the introduction of intruder operations. Mosquito F.Mk.II DZ238 was delivered to No.23 Squadron as YP-H on 9 December 1942 for service in Malta. It made the last Mk.II sortie with the squadron on 17 August 1943.**

Right: **Mosquito F.II DD673 YP-E of No.23 Squadron had an argument with a steam roller at Manston after an engine failure. It was however repaired and returned to service.**

The squadron joined Bomber Command on bomber support operations, intercepting enemy night fighters. After the war the squadron disbanded at Little Snoring on 25 September 1945, but reformed in Fighter Command at Wittering on 11 September 1946, still in the night role. It equipped with Mosquito NF.30s which were later replaced by NF.36s, and then replaced by Vampire night fighters from October 1951.

Right: **Mosquito Mk.II DZ230 YP-A of No.23 Squadron flown by the CO, Wing Commander Wykeham-Barnes over Malta. This was the first Mosquito to see action in Malta on 27 December 1942.**

Below: **No.23 Squadron moved from Malta to Italy following the Allied landings continuing intruder operations over northern Italy. By this time the CO was Wing Commander P Burton Gyles DSO, DFC*.**

Below: **After the war, No.23 Squadron continued as part of the night defence of Britain with the ultimate RAF Mosquito night fighter, the NF36, of which RL206 was an example, based at Coltishall.**

25

SQUADRON

Code Letters:

ZK

Usage:
Mosquito NF.II
Oct 1942 – Mar 1944
Mosquito FB.VI
Aug – Sept 1943,
Jan – Feb 1945
Mosquito NF.XVII
Dec 1943 – Nov 1944
Mosquito NF.30
Sep 1944 – Sep 1946
Mosquito NF.36
Sep 1946 – Sep 1951

Bases:

Church Fenton 5.42 – 12.43
Acklington 12.43 – 2.44
Coltishall 2.44 – 10.44
Castle Camps 10.44 – 7.45
Bradwell Bay 7 – 8.45
Castle Camps 8.45 – 6.46
Boxted 6 – 9.46
West Malling 9.46 – 1957

Above: **Mosquito FB.VI 'E' of No.25 Squadron at Little Snoring; 1944. (George Stewart)**

Below: **By 1950 No.25 Squadron was part of the night defence of Great Britain equipped with Mosquito NF.36s at West Malling, RL123:G being an example. (G A Heather)**

Below: **A somewhat damaged Mosquito F.II DZ696 of No.27 Squadron in 1943 with the Merlin engines and other parts being salvaged before the remainder is scrapped. (RAF Museum)**

27

SQUADRON

Usage:
Mosquito F.II
Apr – Jun 1943
Mosquito FB VI
Dec 1943 – Apr 1944

Bases:

Agartala, India, 2.43 – 2.44
Parashuram, 2 .44 - 4.44

Usage:
Mosquito NF.XII
May 1943 – Apr 1944
Mosquito NF.XIII
Oct 1943 – Feb 1945
Mosquito NF.30
Feb.1945 – 1946
Oct 1950 – Dec 1950
Mosquito NF.36
1946 – Oct 1950

Bases:

Bradwell Bay 5.43 – 9.43
Ford 9.43 – 3.44
Drem 3.44 – 5.44
West Malling 5.44 – 6.44
Hunsdon 6.44 – 2.45
Colerne 2.45 – 4.45
Manston 4.45 – 10.45
West Malling 10.45 – 10.50

Above: **A No.29 Squadron Intruder Mosquito FB.VI returns to Hunsdon after a sortie.**

No.25 Squadron

Service history: Mosquito NF.IIs began to replace Beaufighters in October 1942, with the first combat patrol on 14 November. The first success with Mosquitos was on 16 January 1943 when Flight Lieutenant Singleton in DD752 damaged a Do.217. The squadron then commenced *Rangers*, night sweeps over the Continent, scoring their first train in April. Mosquito FB.VIs began to equip a new 'C Flight' in August for these offensive operations. A detachment to Predannack covered the defence of Coastal Command patrols against enemy attacks. In September 'A Flight' installed Mk.IV AI radar for bomber support duties, later taken over by 100 Group. The squadron specialised in this type of operation until the end of the year when re-equipped with Mosquito NF.XVIIs. In March the squadron claimed nine successes, switching to intruder patrols until the V-1 flying bombs started indiscriminate attacks, when No.25 Squadron moved to night interception of the Doodle-bugs. In support of the Allied invasion of Europe, the squadron was employed on interception and intruder patrols over Europe until the last night of the war when, unfortunately, Flight Lieuenant Jones and Flying Officer Skinner were lost in Mosquito NF.30 MV530. In peace time the squadron was allocated to home defence night fighting at West Malling, equipping with the ultimate Mosquito night fighter to see service with the RAF, the NF36. These remained until July 1951, when No.25 Squadron was responsible for introducing the Vampire NF.10. into RAF service.

No.27 Squadron

Service history: The first Mosquito F.II was delivered to the squadron in April 1943 for operational trials alongside the Beaufighters. At the end of the year 'A Flight' was equipped with Mosquito FB.VIs complimenting the Beaufighter Mk.Xs, allowing day and night operations. The Mosquitos were withdrawn in April 1944 when the squadron joined with No.47 Squadron as a Beaufighter equipped anti-shipping wing. During the period of service with FB.VIs, the commanding officer was Wing Commander J B Nicholson VC, the only Fighter Command VC of World War 2, which he was awarded in the Battle of Britain when he was flying Hurricanes.

Above: **Crews of No.29 Squadron at readiness at Hunsdon in September 1944 in typical accommodation.**

29 Squadron

Service history: In May 1943, No.29 Squadron began replacing its night fighter Beaufighters with Mosquito NF.XIIs, becoming operational again in August, and soon scoring against a Ju88. By November, the squadron had claimed its 60th enemy aircraft at night, but the role changed in 1944 to intruder operations from 14 May. Anti-diver patrols were flown against V-1 flying bombs between October and November, followed by re-equipment with NF.30s in the early part of 1945. It was with one of the new aircraft that Warrant Officer Dallinson destroyed an Me262 jet, and damaged another on 24 April. This was the last action of the war for the squadron and it became part of Fighter Command night fighter defences based at West Malling. This continued until October 1950 when the squadron moved to Tangmere to introduce the Meteor NF.11, becoming the RAF's first jet night fighter unit.

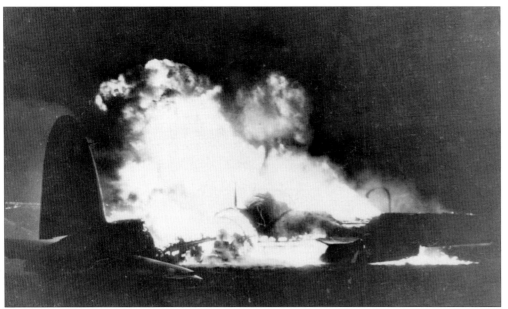

Left: **Although the Mosquito was largely made from wood, it did not always burn this easily. This No.29 Squadron aircraft crashed on return to Hunsdon from a sortie in 1944, but the crew were unhurt.**

Right: **Mosquito NF.XIII HK428 'K' of No.29 Squadron** fitted with a thimble radome housing AI Mk.VIII radar. This aircraft joined No.29 Squadron on 28 January 1944, the crew destroying a Ju88 six months later. The aircraft later served with the Central Gunnery School.

Right: **Leavesden built Mosquito NF.Mk.XIII HK382 RO-T of No.29 Squadron** at dispersal at Hunsdon.

Below: **No.29 Squadron** became part of the UK night defence force based at West Malling in 1947 with Mosquito NF.30s, NT245 being an example.

36
SQUADRON
Code Letters:
DM

Usage:
Mosquito FB.VI
Oct 1946 – Oct 1947

Bases:

Thorney Island 10.46 – 10.47

Above: **On 1 October 1946 No.36 Squadron reformed at Thorney Island by renumbering No.248 Squadron. It was probably the last of the Mosquito coastal strike squadrons when it disbanded at Thorney Island on 15 October 1947. The squadron operated Mosquito FB.VIs similar to NT193 shown here on a test flight from Hatfield in April 1944.**

Below: **No.39 Squadron reformed in the fighter bomber role on 1 March 1949 at Khartoum equipped with Tempest Mk.6s, but transferred to the Canal Zone the following year with Mosquito NF.36s. Operating in the Canal Zone from 1949, it provided night fighter defence with Mosquito NF.36s It remained the sole Middle East night fighter squadron for many years and re-equipped with Meteor NF.13s in November 1952. Mosquito NF.36 RL151 was similar to aircraft with the unit.**

39
SQUADRON

Usage:
Mosquito NF.36
1949 – Nov 1952

Bases:

Khartoum 3.49 – 1949
Fayid 1949 – 1951
Kabrit 1951 – 1.55

45

SQUADRON
Code Letters:

OB

Usage:
Mosquito FB.VI
Feb 1944 – May 1946

Bases:

India 2.44 – 5.46
Negombo, Ceylon 5.46 – 5.49

Above: **Mosquito FB.VIs of No.45 Squadron with Liberators at Santa Cruz in February 1946.**

Above: **Mosquito FB.VI TE879:B being refuelled at Negombo in April 1947.**

Service history: No.45 Squadron converted from Vengeance dive-bombers to Mosquito FB.VIs from January 1944 at Yelahanka in India. The squadron operated from various airfields against the Japanese, dropping a total of 3,144 50lb H E bombs and 90 250lb incendiaries. In May 1946 a move was made to Ceylon in the maritime strike role, re-equipping with Beaufighters in December of the same year.

Below: **Mosquito FB.VI RF957 OB-B of No.45 Squadron at Santa Cruz in 1946.**

46 SQUADRON

Usage:
Mosquito NF.XII
Aug – Dec.44

Bases:

Idku, Egypt
5.42 – 12.44

Above: **The de Havilland Canada built Mosquito FB.XXVI was generally similar to the British built example, but used local materials in its construction, and was powered by Packard built Merlin engines. After having a new gun fitted, a Mosquito FB.VI shows the destructive power of the four machine guns and four cannons, and is similar to the FB.XXVIs operated by No.55 Squadron around the Aegean Sea until November 1946.**

Service history: In August 1944 No.46 Squadron began to replace Beaufighters with Mosquito NF.XIIs at Idku in Egypt with detachments around Egypt, North Africa and Cyprus. In September, during a detachment at Gambut, eleven enemy aircraft were destroyed in five days while intruding in the Aegean. With the withdrawal of enemy aircraft from Greece in November, the squadron returned to Britain in December 1944, becoming a transport unit.

Below: **Mosquito FB.VIs of No.47 Squadron operated on the Arakan front in Burma. The Mosquitos gradually replaced rocket firing ground attack Beaufighters at Kumbhirgram in India, before moving to Kinmagan in Burma for operations against the Japanese. The aircraft were fitted with RP carriers under the wings for operations against the Indonesian Nationalists in Java operating from Butterworth, until disbanding in March 1946.**

47 SQUADRON

Code Letters:

KU

Usage:
Mosquito FB.VI
Feb.45 – Mar.46

Bases:

India 2.45 – 4.45
Burma 4.45 – 1.46
Butterworth, Malaya
1.46 – 3.46

55 SQUADRON

Usage:
Mosquito FB.XXVI
Jul – Nov.46

Bases:

Hassani Greece
9.45 – 11.46

Above: **An intruder crew boarding their aircraft through the hatch.**

68
SQUADRON
Code Letters:
WM

Usage:
Mosquito NF.XVII
Jul 1944 – Feb 1945
Mosquito NF.XIX
Jul 1944 – Feb 1945
Mosquito NF.30
Feb – Apr 1945

Bases:

Castle Camps 6 – 10.44
Coltishall 10.44 – 2.45
Wittering 2.45
Coltishall 2 – 3.45
Church Fenton 3 – 4.45

Service history: Mosquitos replaced Beaufighters in the night fighter role in July 1944 and were soon flying anti diver patrols against V-1s. The squadron was also sent out over the North Sea after Heinkel He111s used to air-launch V-1s, claiming its first success against one of these combinations on 5 November. With the advance of the invading Allied forces across Europe, the UK based night fighter force was reduced and 68 Squadron disbanded on 20 April 1945.

Above: **Warrant Officer Fridolín Gemrod (Radio Operator) relaxes at Castle Camps on the tail of Mosquito NF Mk.XVII WM-G during the summer of 1944. (Z. Hurt)**

Right: **A farewell photo taken at Church Fenton around 20 April 1945, the official date of No.68´s disbandment. In the front row centre is Wing Commander L W Gill with 'B' Flight commander Squadron Leader Wright (left) and 'A' Flight commander Squadron Leader M Mansfeld DFC. (Z. Hurt)**

69
SQUADRON
Code Letters:
WI

Usage:
Mosquito FB.VI
Aug 1945 – Nov 1947
Mosquito B.XVI
Apr 1946 – Nov 1947

Bases:

Cambrai/Epinoy,
France 8.45 – 3.46
Wahn, Germany
4.46 – 11.47

Above: **Mosquito FB.VI RF773 UX-P of No.82 Squadron at St Thomas Mount, Madras in January 1946.**
The squadron replaced its Vultee Vengeance in the dive bomber role with Mosquito FB.VIs in July 1944,

Left: **The return of Mosquito FB.VI UX-T of No.82 Squadron along the taxi way after a sortie from St Thomas Mount, Madras in January 1946.**

Below: **Standard Motors built Mosquito FB.VI HR493 UX-C of No.82 Squadron in Burma in 1945. Intruder operations were flown in Burma until withdrawn in June 1945.**

82
SQUADRON
Code Letters:
UX

Usage:
Mosquito FB.VI
Jul 1944 – Mar 1946

Bases:

Kolar, India 6.44 – 10.44
Ranchi 10.44 – 12.44
Chharra 12.44
Kumbhirgram 12.44 – 4.45
Chotavaram 5.45 – 10.45
Madras 10.45 – 3.46

Above: **A No.84 Squadron Mosquito FB.VI flown by Flying Officer Johnson with Flying Officer Jenkins as navigator over Malaya in March 1946.**

Below: **Mosquito FB.VI TE616 of No.84 Squadron in close formation over Malaya.**

Service history: In July 1944, No.84 Squadron was taken off operations with Vengeance aircraft to convert to Mosquitos, but due to technical problems, the Mosquitos were not used against the Japanese. In September 1945 the squadron moved to Seletar before moving to Java, where it operated until mid 1946. No.84 Squadron operated around SE Asia including Singapore and Malaya against the rebels in the Netherlands East Indies, re-equipping with Beaufighters in December 1946 for operations against the Malayan terrorists.

Left: **Mosquito FB.VIs of No.84 Squadron at Kuala Lumpur in 1946.**
(B T Thomas)

85

SQUADRON

Code Letters:

VY

Usage:
Mosquito NF.II
Aug 1942 – May 1943
Mosquito NF.XV
Mar 1943 – 1943
Mosquito NF.XII
Mar 1943 – 1944
Mosquito NF.XVII
Nov 1943 – 1944
Mosquito NF.30
Nov 1944 – 1947
Mosquito NF.36
1947 – Oct 1951

Bases:

Hunsdon 5.41 – 5.43
West Malling 5.43 – 5.44
Swannington 4.44 – 7.44
West Malling 7.44 – 8.44
Swannington 8.44 – 1945
Colerne 1945 – 9.46
Tangmere 9.46 – 1947
West Malling 1947 – 9.57

Above: **The wartime censor touched out the arrow head AI antennas on these two Mosquito NF.IIs of No.85 Squadron. (DH Photo)**

Below: **On the night of 24–25 March 1944, Flying Officer Hedgecoe of No.85 Squadron destroyed a Ju188. When he hit the raider, there was a large explosion. Debris and fuel engulfed the Mosquito, burning off the fabric covering.**

26

Right: **Mosquitos replaced Havocs from August 1942 and in January 1943, John Cunningham joined the squadron as the commanding officer to supervise the introduction of the improved Mosquito NF.XIIs and to operate the specially adapted high altitude Mk.XVs against high flying German nuisance raiders. This example is HK117 illustrated in March 1943 after modification by Marshall of Cambridge.**

With reduced enemy night activity, No.85 Squadron formed an extra flight for intruder patrols as well as operating the Mk.XVs up to 43,000ft. With the new NF.XIIs it accounted for four FW190s, with one probable, in one night, the first FW190s to be destroyed at night over the UK. The squadron remained busy throughout the rest of the year, with ten successes in October and the total score reaching 200 in January 1944. On 1 May 1944, the squadron transferred to 100 Group, Bomber Command for bomber support work, initially in the form of low level intruding over German airfields. At the start of the V-1 offensive, No.85 Squadron was allocated to anti-diver patrols.

Right: **Mosquito NF.30 MV548 VY-Y of No.85 Squadron on dispersal at Colerne in 1945 with the print signed by the crew.**

With the end of the war in Europe, the squadron returned to Fighter Command as part of night fighter defence, spending most of the time at West Malling where it re-equipped with Meteor NF.11s in October 1951.

Right: **No.85 Squadron Mosquito NF.36s at Coltishall on 28 September 1951, including RL174:E with the post war unit markings.**
(M C Gray)

John Cunningham
Night Fighter

Although the Mosquito was not the first dedicated night fighter in World War Two equipped with the then secret Airborne Interception (AI) Radar, it was certainly the most effective. John Cunningham, the WW2 night fighter ace, had gained his earlier victories using AI equipped Beaufighters with No.604 Squadron RAuxAF based at Middle Wallop, which is still active as a grass airfield and the home of Army Aviation.

The Mosquito, although originally conceived as an unarmed bomber, was an ideal night fighter platform with a good load carrying capability for the heavy radar equipment, good endurance for long night patrols and room for two crew – a pilot and radar operator/navigator. In addition the aircraft was highly manoeuvrable with a high top speed to allow it to catch up with enemy raiders and position for the successful interception.

Mosquito night fighters first entered service with No.157 Squadron at Debden under the command of Wing Commander Gordon Slade in December 1941, moving to Castle Camps the following month. The early aircraft were fully equipped apart from the radar, but AI equipped Mosquitos began to arrive in April 1942. No.151 Squadron received the first Mosquito NF.II at Wittering in April to replace the unsatisfactory Defiants. Following conversion to the new type crews practised interceptions in pairs, taking it in turns to be target and attacker. Training and operations included close co-operation with the ground radar controllers, who vectored the Mosquitos to within AI radar range of their targets.

Wing Commander John Cunningham took over as Commanding Officer of No.85 Squadron at Hunsdon on 27 January 1943. He had learned to fly with No.604 Squadron RAuxAF at Hendon, making his first solo on 15 March 1936 while serving with the de Havilland Aeronautical Technical School at Hatfield. Soon after graduating he joined the test pilot team at Hatfield sharing the test flying with Geoffrey de Havilland Jnr on the Moth Minor programme.

With war approaching, John was mobilised as a night fighter pilot with No.604 Squadron flying Blenheim 1Fs over the North Sea. Following the Battle of Britain, the first operational aircraft to be fitted with AI radar were the night fighters of No.604 Squadron. On the night of 20/21 November 1940, flying a Blenheim, John successfully intercepted using AI radar and shot down a German Ju88 as it crossed the Sussex Coast; a world first.

Soon after that No.604 Squadron converted to the higher performance Beaufighters, allowing John and his radar operator, Jimmy Rawnsley, to develop and perfect the techniques of working with the ground controllers to within range of the raiders. Once acquired on the AI set, the crew

Above: John Cunningham and Jimmy Rawnsley were a successful night fighter team, operating first the AI equipped Beaufighters with No.604 Squadron at Middle Wallop, followed by Mosquito night fighters with No.85 Squadron at Hunsdon. This team achieved twenty confirmed successes against enemy raiders, with three probables and six damaged. John was awarded the DSO and DFC* for his exploits.**

Right: **John gained experience on Hawker Demons with No.604 Squadron at Hendon after he had gained his wings. With mobilisation, the squadron was re-equipped with Blenheims, before converting to the more effective Beaufighter night fighters.**

stalked the enemy aircraft, approaching from behind and below to positively identify it as a hostile aircraft, preferably before it had time to drop its bomb load. Identification was essential to ensure that it was not an Allied aircraft flying around. John would then drop back and climb to behind the German aircraft before firing a burst of cannon fire into the rear of whatever type had been detected. This process was not without its hazards, as debris often flew off the enemy aircraft, causing damage to the attacker. While the air cooled radial engine Beaufighter was often tough enough to withstand this damage, the Mosquito with its water cooled Merlin engines and wing leading edge radiators could be more vulnerable.

In February 1941 John was invited by Sir Geoffrey de Havilland with the approval of Air Chief Marshal Sir Charles Portal, to fly the Mosquito Prototype W4050. He was the first RAF pilot to fly the Mosquito and strongly recommended its development as a night fighter. The Interim Mosquito NF.II and more effective NF.XII resulted. In the Spring of 1941 John achieved five more successes, three in one night, and in May he shot down a Heinkel for the benefit of HRH King George VI, who was observing

operations from a ground radar station. Because the use of AI radar was highly classified, the media gave John the nickname of "Cat's eyes" with the suggestion that he ate carrots to help him see in the dark. John did in fact have exceptional eyesight, but the use of AI was essential to track and identify targets.

In July 1942, Wing Commander John Cunningham was appointed commanding officer of No.85 Squadron at

Below: **In the autumn of 1941 as a very young Wing Commander, John was appointed the commanding officer of No.604 Squadron at Middle Wallop flying Beaufighter night fighters.**

Below: **John examining the crest of No.85 Squadron on his appointment as CO in March 1943.**

29

Left: **In the summer of 1942 John relaxes with his colleagues at Middle Wallop. From left to right is John, Jack Foster, George McLannahan, Per Bugge, Bob Wright and Jeremy Howard Williams. Per Bugge, more commonly known as Peter Bugge, joined the test pilot team with de Havilland at Hatfield after the war as John's deputy. Peter had escaped from his native Norway by sea to join the RAF.**

Hunsdon, initially equipped with Mosquito NF.IIs, but later to introduce the more effective NF.XIIs to operational service. John had a nasty surprise when approaching to identify a Ju188, which he did not know had a rear gunner. Some well aimed shots hit his bullet-proof windscreen, showering him with particles of glass. He broke off the engagement and landed the damaged aircraft at West Malling, later being presented with the broken windscreen. John's Mosquito was later hit by wreckage from an FW190, the Luftwaffe's fastest propeller fighter, which he had caught and destroyed. John was appointed Group Captain, one of the youngest in the RAF, at the age of 27 in charge of night fighting operations in 11 Group in January 1944 with a total of twenty confirmed night fighting success. His awards included three DSOs and two DFCs. Although he was destined for a successful career in the RAF, he elected to return to de Havilland at Hatfield as a test pilot, later to become the chief test pilot and pioneered jet travel with testing the Comet. John died in July 2002, just a few days before his 85th birthday.

Left: **On his appointment as CO of No.85 Squadron at Hunsdon in March 1943, John was congratulated by AVM H Saunders (right).**

89
SQUADRON

Usage:
Mosquito FB.VI
Feb 1945 - Apr 1946
Mosquito NF.XIX
May 1945 - Apr 1946

Bases:

Balgachi, India 8.44 – 9.45
Hmawbi 9.45
Seletar 9.45 – 5.46

Above: **Mosquito FB.VIs and NF.XIXs were used by No. 89 Squadron in India and later Seletar, Singapore, replacing Beau-fighters between February and July 1945. This FB.VI is seen taxying in typical monsoon conditions and is similar to those used by No.89 Squadron. The squadron did not become operational with the Mosquitos, but flew leaflet sorties over the Dutch Islands from Seletar. In April 1946 the unit was rundown and renumbered No.22 Squadron on 1 May 1946.**

Below: **Mosquito NF.XIII HK419 ZJ-B of No. 96 Squadron at West Malling in 1943. Mosquitos began to replace Beaufighters in June 1943 and were used on regular night patrols. The first success came on 2nd January 1944, when Flight Lieutenant Head destroyed an FW190. This was followed two nights later by the commanding officer, Wing Commander E D Crew, claiming an Me410 destroyed and damaging another. The squadron continued to score until June, when it was allocated to anti-diver patrols, claiming 49 V-1s in the month. The squadron was disbanded at Odiham on 12 December 1944 with the V-1 menace overcome and reduced enemy air activity over Britain at night.**

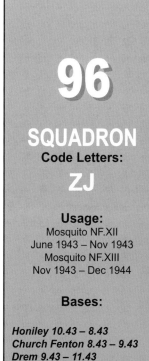

96
SQUADRON
Code Letters:
ZJ

Usage:
Mosquito NF.XII
June 1943 – Nov 1943
Mosquito NF.XIII
Nov 1943 – Dec 1944

Bases:

Honiley 10.43 – 8.43
Church Fenton 8.43 – 9.43
Drem 9.43 – 11.43
West Malling 11.43 – 6.44
Ford 6.44 – 9.44
Odiham 9.44 – 12.44

Usage:
Mosquito FB.VI
Feb 1944 – Oct 1948

Bases:

Lasham 2.44 – 10.44
Blackbushe 10.44 – 11.44
Cambrai 11.44 – 7.45
Brussels 7.45 – 11.45
Gutersloh 11.45 – 11.47
Wahn 11.47 – 10.48.

Above: **Ground crew wave from Mosquito FB.VI TA118, while preparing it for flight. (J E Bilbrough)** No. 107 Squadron specialised in low level precision raids, replacing Bostons with Mosquitos in February 1944. At the end of the war the squadron became part of the British Air Forces of Occupation (BAFO), and renumbered No. 11 Squadron in October 1948.

Below: **Mosquito FB.VIs of Nos. 21 and 107 Squadrons at Gutersloh in 1947. The aircraft include HR358:OM-B. The armoured car protection is from the RAF Regiment. (A Thomas)**

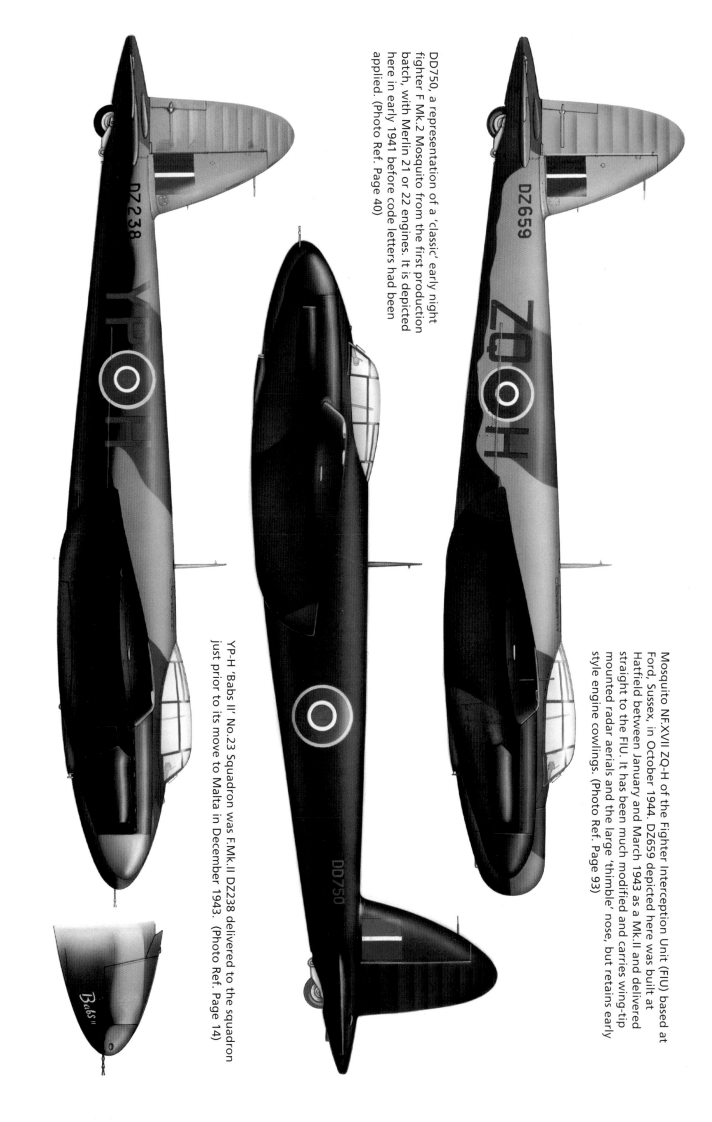

DD750, a representation of a 'classic' early night fighter F Mk.2 Mosquito from the first production batch, with Merlin 21 or 22 engines. It is depicted here in early 1941 before code letters had been applied. (Photo Ref. Page 40)

YP-H 'Babs II' No.23 Squadron was F.Mk.II DZ238 delivered to the squadron just prior to its move to Malta in December 1943. (Photo Ref. Page 14)

Mosquito NF.XVII ZQ-H of the Fighter Interception Unit (FIU) based at Ford, Sussex, in October 1944. DZ659 depicted here was built at Hatfield between January and March 1943 as a Mk.II and delivered straight to the FIU. It has been much modified and carries wing-tip mounted radar aerials and the large 'thimble' nose, but retains early style engine cowlings. (Photo Ref. Page 93)

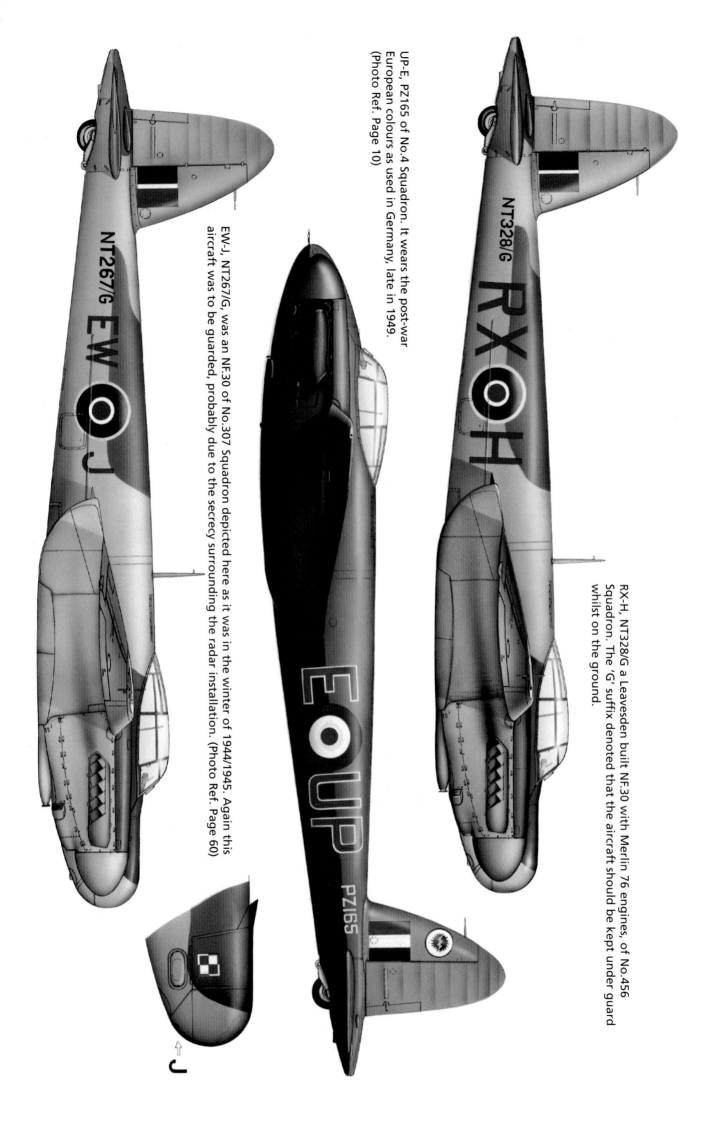

UP-E, PZ165 of No.4 Squadron. It wears the post-war
European colours as used in Germany, late in 1949.
(Photo Ref. Page 10)

RX-H, NT328/G a Leavesden built NF.30 with Merlin 76 engines, of No.456
Squadron. The 'G' suffix denoted that the aircraft should be kept under guard
whilst on the ground.

EW-J, NT267/G, was an NF.30 of No.307 Squadron depicted here as it was in the winter of 1944/1945. Again this
aircraft was to be guarded, probably due to the secrecy surrounding the radar installation. (Photo Ref. Page 60)

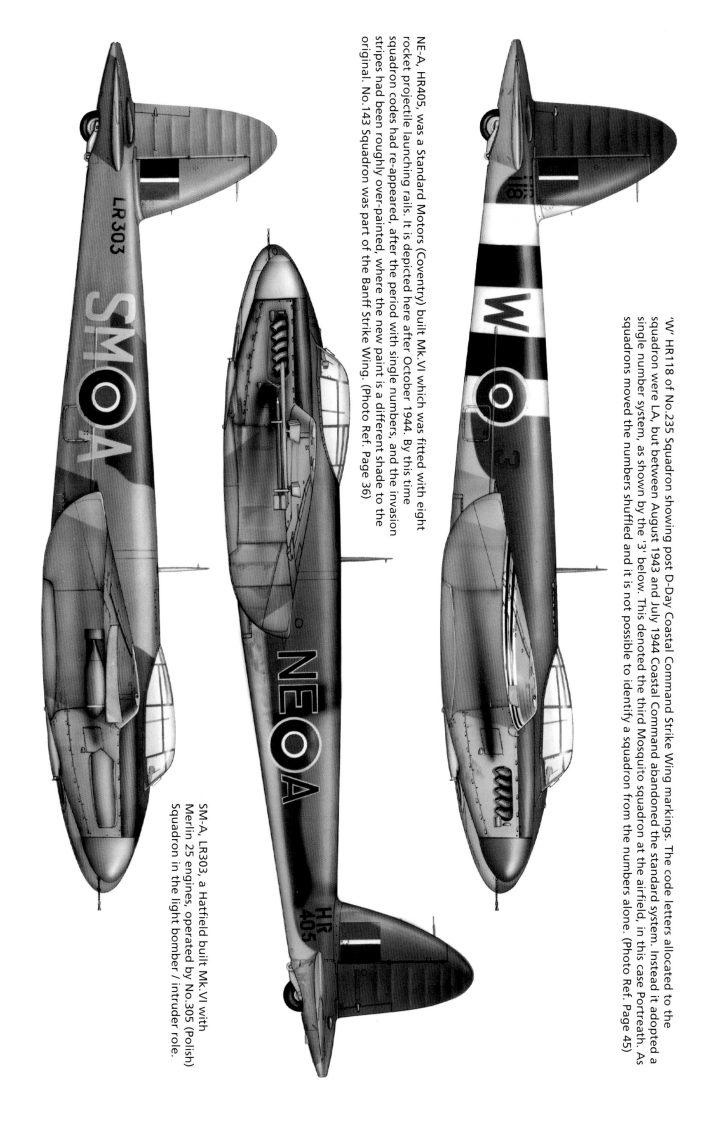

'W' HR118 of No.235 Squadron showing post D-Day Coastal Command Strike Wing markings. The code letters allocated to the squadron were LA, but between August 1943 and July 1944 Coastal Command abandoned the standard system. Instead it adopted a single number system, as shown by the '3' below. This denoted the third Mosquito squadron at the airfield, in this case Portreath. As squadrons moved the numbers shuffled and it is not possible to identify a squadron from the numbers alone. (Photo Ref. Page 45)

NE-A, HR405, was a Standard Motors (Coventry) built Mk.VI which was fitted with eight rocket projectile launching rails. It is depicted here after October 1944. By this time squadron codes had re-appeared, after the period with single numbers, and the invasion stripes had been roughly over-painted, where the new paint is a different shade to the original. No.143 Squadron was part of the Banff Strike Wing. (Photo Ref. Page 36)

SM-A, LR303, a Hatfield built Mk.VI with Merlin 25 engines, operated by No.305 (Polish) Squadron in the light bomber / intruder role.

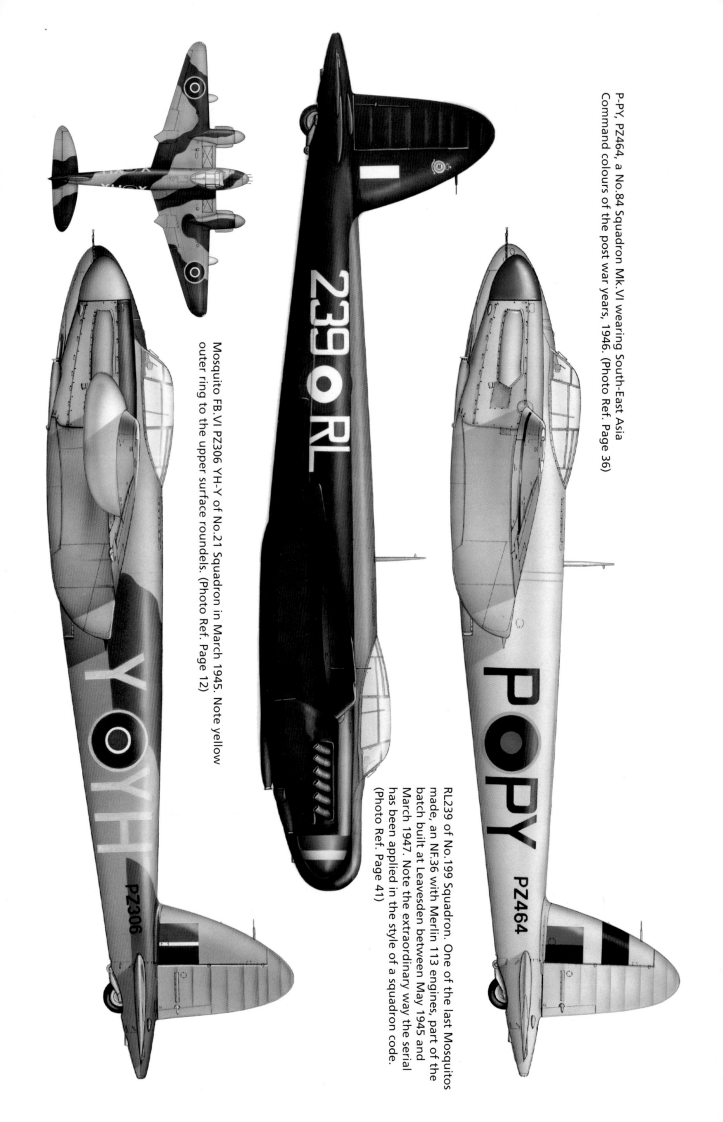

P-PY, PZ464, a No.84 Squadron Mk.VI wearing South-East Asia
Command colours of the post war years, 1946. (Photo Ref. Page 36)

Mosquito FB.VI PZ306 YH-Y of No.21 Squadron in March 1945. Note yellow
outer ring to the upper surface roundels. (Photo Ref. Page 12)

RL239 of No.199 Squadron. One of the last Mosquitos
made, an NF.36 with Merlin 113 engines, part of the
batch built at Leavesden between May 1945 and
March 1947. Note the extraordinary way the serial
has been applied in the style of a squadron code.
(Photo Ref. Page 41)

108
SQUADRON

Usage:
Mosquito NF.XII
Feb 1944 – May 1944
Mosquito NF.XIII
Mar 1944 – July 1944

Bases:

Luqa, Malta 6.44 – 7.44
Hal Far 7.44

Left: **No. 108 Squadron was equipped with Mosquito NF.XIIs and XIIIs and based at Malta during 1944. NF.XIII MM478 is similar to those used by the squadron. In February 1944 the squadron began to convert to Mosquito night fighters from Beaufighters. Mosquito operations commenced in March with convoy patrols followed by intruder operations, before being sent to Egypt in July and relinquishing its Mosquitos.**

Below: **Mosquito FB.VI TA230:N, believed to have served with No. 110 Squadron at Singapore. Mosquito FB.VIs began to replace Vengeances from November 1944, the re-equipment being completed by January 1945 for ground attack duties against Japanese troops. In fact eight Mosquitos with No. 110 Squadron made an attack on some still warlike Japanese troops on 20 August 1945 east of the Sittang River. This was six days after the unconditional surrender and five days after VJ Day. This was the last RAF offensive against the Japanese. A detachment of the squadron operated against the Indonesian terrorists before the squadron was disbanded on 15 April 1946.**

110
SQUADRON
Code Letters:
VE

Usage:
Mosquito FB.VI
Nov 1944 – Apr 1946

Bases:

Yellanka, India 10.44 – 5.45
Joari 3.45 – 5.45
Kinmagan, Burma 5.45 – 8.45
Hmawbi 8.45 – 10.45
Seletar 10.45 – 2.46
Labuan, Borneo 2.46 – 4.46.

114
SQUADRON
Code Letters:
RT

Usage:
Mosquito FB.VI
Sept 1945 - Sept 1946

Bases:

Khormaksar, Aden
9.45 – 9.46

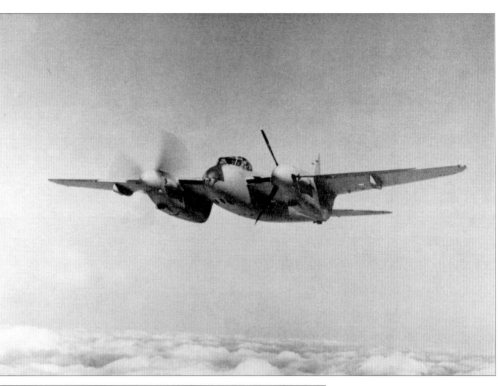

Right: **No.114 Squadron operated Mosquitos in Aden for a year on peace keeping duties. The squadron assisted in maintaining the peace in Aden until 1 September 1946 when it was renumbered No.8 Squadron.**

Left: **Mosquito NF.30 of No. 125 Squadron with large nose mounted radome to protect the improved AI.**

Below: **Mosquito NF.30s of No. 125 Squadron lined up at Church Fenton in 1945.**

Service history: In early 1944 No.125 Squadron began to convert from Beaufighters to Mosquitos at Valley, and moved to Hurn in March, where it found action almost every night. With the Allied invasion in June, the squadron operated standing patrols in support of the ground forces, and went over to anti-diver patrols in September with the first success on 25 September. The last victory for No. 125 Squadron was on 20 March 1945 when an enemy aircraft was shot down into the sea and the squadron had claimed a total of 44 aircraft destroyed, five probables and 20 damaged. The squadron remained in Fighter Command until 20 November 1945, when it disbanded at Church Fenton.

125
SQUADRON
Code Letters:
VA

Usage:
Mosquito FB.XVII
Feb 1944 – Mar 1945
Mosquito NF.30
Mar 1945 - Nov 1945

Bases:

Valley 11.43 – 3.44
Hurn 3.44 – 7.44
Middle Wallop 7.44 – 10.44
Coltishall 10.44 – 4.45
Church Fenton 4.45 – 11.45

141

SQUADRON
Code Letters:
TW

Usage:
Mosquito NF.II
Nov 1942 – Aug 1944
Mosquito FB.VI
Aug 1944 - Apr 1945
Mosquito NF.30
Apr 1945 - Sept 1945
Mosquito NF.36
June 1946 - Sept 1951

Bases:

Wittering 4.43 – 12.43
West Raynham 12.43 – 7.45
Little Snoring 7.45 – 9.45
Coltishall 6.46 – 11.49
Church Fenton 11.49 – 9.50
Coltishall 9.50 – 1.58.

Above: **Leavesden built Mosquito NF.36 RL239 TW-D of No.141 Squadron at Coltishall in January 1951. (R A Brown)**

Below: **The ultimate piston engine RAF night fighter Mosquito NF.36 RL239 TW-D of No.141 Squadron. From early 1943, the squadron used Beaufighters on intruder work, which were replaced by Mosquitos from November. In December, the squadron joined 100 Group on bomber support duties, but continued intruding until a conversion was made to NF.30s from April 1945. April was a busy month, but the last operational sortie was flown on 2 May, 1945. The squadron remained in existence until disbanding at Little Snoring on 7 September 1945, after VJ Day. No. 141 Squadron reformed at Coltishall on 17 June 1946 within Fighter Command with NF.36s until they were replaced with Meteor NF.11s from September 1951.**

143

SQUADRON

Code Letters:

NE

Usage:
Mosquito FB.VI
Oct 1944 - May 1945

Bases:

Banff 10.44 – 5.45

Right: **As part of the Banff Strike Wing, No.143 Squadron was involved in anti-shipping operations along the Norwegian coastline and around Denmark. Mosquito FB.VI HR405 NE-A of No.143 Squadron armed with eight underwing RP in addition to the normal fixed gun armament.**

Below: **Armourers and ground crew load RP on to the underwing rails of a No.143 Squadron Mosquito FB.VI.**

Above and below: **Mosquito FB.VI RS625 NE-D of No. 143 Squadron fitted with underwing fuel drop tanks and the revised launchers for RP. The crew of this aircraft, Squadron Leader David Pritchard and Flight Lieutenant W Bower were responsible for the sinking of U-804 on 9 April 1945, amongst other shipping targets.**

Service history: Used for anti-shipping strikes as part of the Banff Strike Wing, the squadron moved from North Coates in October 1944, replacing its Beaufighters with Mosquitos. The operational areas included Norwegian coastal waters, the main armament being underwing mounted RP. The squadron shared in the destruction of four U-boats in the Skagerrak and Kattegat, and on 21 April destroyed five Ju88s and four Ju188s out of a formation of 18 enemy aircraft. The last action was a strike on Kiel on 3 May 1945, with ASR patrols following until it was disbanded by being renumbered No.14 Squadron on 25 May 1945.

Usage:
Mosquito NF.II
Apr 1942 – July 1943
Mosquito NF.XII
June 1943 – 1944
Mosquito NF.XIII
Dec 1943 – Sept 1944
Mosquito FB.VI
July 1944 - Sept 1944
Mosquito NF.30
Sept 1944 – Oct 1946

Bases:

Wittering 12.40 – 4.43
Colerne 4.43 – 8.43
Middle Wallop 8.43 – 11.43
Colerne 11.43 – 3.44
Predannack 3.44 – 10.44
Castle Camps 10.44 – 11.44
Hunsdon 11.44 – 3.45
Bradwell Bay 3.45 – 5.45
Predannack 5.45 – 6.46
Exeter 6.43 – 9.46
Colerne 9.46
Weston Zoyland 10.46.

Above: **No.151 Squadron began replacing Turbinlite Havocs with the more effective Mosquito NF.IIs similar to DD609 shown featuring the nose antenna.**

Below: **A Turbinlite Mosquito, W4087 being an example, was evaluated by No.151 Squadron in December 1942 to follow on from the use of Havocs; this also was found ineffective.**

Left: **Mosquito FB.VI of No.151 Squadron at Predannack in 1945. (DHAHC collection)**

Below: **The scene at a dispersal at Hunsdon, where No.151 Squadron was based towards the end of the war.**

Service history: In April 1942 No. 151 Squadron began to re-equip with Mosquitos from Turbinlite Havocs, with which they had no success. The squadron was operational on the new aircraft by 29 May, when an He111 and Do217 were damaged on the same night. The following month, the squadron began standing patrols over the North Sea, gaining some victories until German raiders became scarce due to the winter weather. In December, the squadron had a Turbinlite Mosquito on loan for trials. In mid February 1943 night intruder patrols over France were started as well as daytime *Rangers*. In July the squadron began to convert to the more capable NF.XIIs, but was only able to claim one victory for the last six months of the year. Operations were moving more to the Western Approaches where victories were claimed against He177s. In March 1944 the unit was allocated to the anti-shipping role and, while on one of these on 11 April, destroyed seven enemy aircraft with the loss of two Mosquitos bringing the squadron's score to 100. The squadron then began to fly night *Rangers* over occupied France, and flew bomber support missions with FB.VIs from July to September 1944, as well as patrols over Belgium and Holland. After the war the squadron returned to the West Country and was disbanded at Weston Zoyland on 10 October 1946.

157

SQUADRON
Code Letters:
RS

Usage:
Mosquito NF.II
Jan 1942 – May 1944
Mosquito NF.XIX
May 1944 - May 1945
Mosquito NF.30
Mar 1945 - Aug 1945

Bases:

Castle Camps 12.41 – 3.43
Bradwell Bay 3.43 – 5.43
Hunsdon 5.43 – 11.43
Predannack 11.43 – 3.44
Valley 3.44 – 5.44
Swannington 5.44 – 7.44
West Malling 7.44 – 8.44
Swannington 8.44 – 8.45

Above: **Mosquito NF.II DD750 on a test flight prior to delivery to the RAF. This aircraft served with No.157 Squadron amongst others including Nos.25, 239 and 264. The matt black finish was eventually discontinued, as it caused additional drag, and was changed to a revised day camouflage scheme.**

Below: **The personnel of No.169 Squadron parade past the saluting base with one of their Mosquito FB.VIs in the background at Little Snoring in 1945. The squadron had been disbanded at Middle Wallop on 1 October 1943, and reformed the same day at Ayr as a night fighter unit with Mosquito NF.IIs. It transferred to 100 Group for bomber support duties in December and became operational on 20 January 1944 with *Serrate* sorties, homing on enemy fighter transmissions and attacking them at night. In May the squadron also began night *Rangers*, destroying enemy aircraft at their own airfields. In October the squadron was almost entirely allocated to intruding, but as the winter nights became longer, *Serrate* patrols were re-introduced. This continued to the squadron's last operation of the war on 2 May when napalm was dropped on German airfields. The squadron was disbanded at Great Massingham on 10 August 1945.**

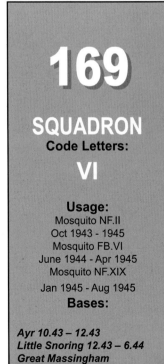

169

SQUADRON
Code Letters:
VI

Usage:
Mosquito NF.II
Oct 1943 - 1945
Mosquito FB.VI
June 1944 - Apr 1945
Mosquito NF.XIX
Jan 1945 - Aug 1945

Bases:

Ayr 10.43 – 12.43
Little Snoring 12.43 – 6.44
Great Massingham
6.44 – 8.45

176
SQUADRON

Usage:

Mosquito NF.XIX
July 1945 – Jan 1946

Bases:

Baigachi, India 3.45 – 6.46

No.157
The First Mosquito Fighter Squadron

157 Squadron was reformed at Debden on 13 December 1941 and was responsible for the introduction of the fighter Mosquito to the RAF. The first aircraft was delivered in January 1942, but the introduction to combat was delayed due to lack of aircraft and poor facilities at Debden. More aircraft were delivered in March, allowing the squadron to be declared operational by 27 April, flying three or more patrols per night. The first score was a probable Do217 by Squadron Leader Ashfield in W4099 on 29 May 1942, with the first confirmed victory being claimed on 22 August by Wing Commander R Gordon Slade with another Do217. During the winter the squadron developed night fighter tactics and in March 1943 began training for intruding, the first *Ranger* being flown on 23 March. A FW190 was shot down at night on 14 May. Predannack was used as an advanced landing ground for anti-fighter patrols over the Bay of Biscay. On bomber support duties, starting in August, the first success was in November when Squadron Leader Robinson claimed a Do217 over Dusseldorf.

Above: **Mosquito NF.XIX TA230 similar to the type operated by No.176 Squadron from July 1945 to January 1946. The squadron was too late to become operational after converting from Beaufighters. The war soon ended and flying ceased in January 1946, followed by disbandment on 1 June 1946.**

Below: **Mosquito NF.36 RL239 of No.199 Squadron at Hemswell in post war markings including an unusual presentation of the serial number. In the background is the Mosquito bomber replacement – the Canberra. The squadron was reformed in July 1951 at the Central Signals Establishment at Watton, equipped with Lincolns and Mosquito NF.36s. These aircraft were used on a radio counter-measures role, and a move was made to Hemswell within 90 Group, Bomber Command in April 1952, soon after which the Mosquitos were retired and later replaced by Canberras.**

199
SQUADRON

Usage:
Mosquito NF.36
1951 - Late 1953

Bases:

Watton 7.51 – 4.52
Hemswell 4.52 – 10.52
Honington 10.52 – 1953

211

SQUADRON

Usage:
Mosquito FB.VI
May 1945 - Feb 1946

Bases:

Yelahanka, India 5.45 – 6.45
St. Thomas Mount
6.45 – 9.45
Cholavarum 9.45 – 11.45
Akyab 11.45
Don Muang, Bangkok
11.45 – 2.46

Right: **Mosquito FB.VIs of No.211 Squadron at Bangkok in November 1945, including RF751:B and RF711:A.**

Below: **Mosquito FB.VI RF819 'K' of No.211 Squadron at Bangkok undergoing maintenance including undercarriage retractions in November 1945.**

Service history: No.211 Squadron converted from Beaufighters to Mosquitos in May 1945, but was not operational before the end of the war. A move was made to Bangkok in November, but following the mid-air break up of one of the Mosquitos in January 1946 the aircraft were grounded. Although the aircraft were given spar inspections, before the squadron could re-commence flying 211 was disbanded at the end of February 1946.

Above: **Mosquito NF.30 NT538 FK-D of No.219 Squadron.**

219

SQUADRON
Code Letters:
FK

Usage:

Mosquito NF.XIII
Feb 1944 – 1944
Mosquito NF.30
1944 - Sept 1946

Bases:

Woodvale 2.44 – 3.44
Honiley 3.44 – 5.44
Bradwell Bay 5.44 – 8.44
Hunsdon 8.44 –10.44
Amiens 10.44 – 3.45
Gilze Rijen, Holland
3.45 – 6.45
Enschede 6.45 – 7.45
Twente 7.45 – 8.45
Acklington 8.45 – 4.46
Wittering 4.46
Acklington – 9.46

Left: **Mosquito T.III TV970 FK-V of No.219 Squadron stored in 1950 after service.**

Service history: The squadron became operational with Mosquito XIIIs at Woodvale in March 1944 with detachments to Colerne and Bradwell Bay. It claimed its first success on 27 March against a Ju88 over Yeovil. Regular night patrols were made over the Channel and occupied Holland and in June the squadron was allocated to anti-diver operations. Following the invasion by the Allies, the squadron provided beach-head patrols and as the ground forces advanced across Europe, the squadron moved to the Continent to keep close to the advance ground forces. The squadron's 100th victory was claimed on 28 September with the destruction of a Ju87 and it provided night cover for the advancing forces throughout the winter until its last victim, an He177, on 9 April 1945. A return was made to Fighter Command in August 1945 and was disbanded at Acklington on 1 September 1946.

Left: **Mosquito NF.30s at Wittering including MM813 and MM806. (E Gosling)**

43

Left: **Mosquito NF.36 RK988 'R' of No.219 Squadron at RAF Kabrit MEAF in 1951. This aircraft was lost in early 1952 while on a low level night air-to-air firing sortie, killing the crew.** (de Havilland Aircraft Heritage Centre (DHAHC) collection)

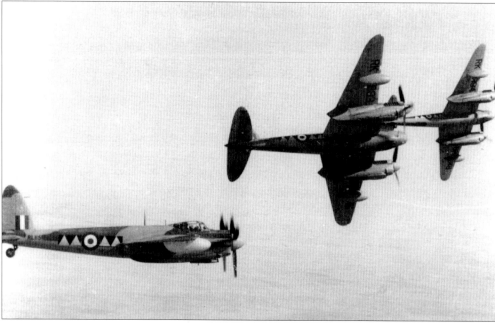

Left: **A formation break of Mosquito NF.36s RL115, RK989 and EK984, based at Kabrit. The photo was used on the No.219 Squadron Christmas card, December 1951. (DHAHC collection)**

Left: **Mosquito NF.36 RL205 'Y' of No.219 Squadron in 1951/52 while based at RAF Kabrit MEAF.** (DHAHC collection)

235

SQUADRON
Code Letters:

LA

Usage:
Mosquito FB.VI
June 1944 - July 1945

Bases:

Portreath 8.43 – 9.44
Banff 9.44 – 7.45

Above: **Standard built Mosquito FB.VI HR118 W-3 of No.235 Squadron at low level over the sea alongside a colleague. Coastal Command aircraft between August 1943 and July 1944 carried no squadron code letters, but a single number, as shown by the '3' above. This denoted the third Mosquito squadron at the airfield, in this case Portreath. As squadrons moved the numbers shuffled. Confusiuon reigned, not just to the enemy, but to everyone involved!**

Above: **Frenchman Wing Commander Max Guedj DSO, DFC* was killed in action while leading 235 and 248 Squadrons on a Mosquito shipping strike in Narvik Fiord in January 1945.**

Above: **Damage to the starboard wing of Mosquito FB.VI HR138 'Y' of No.235 Squadron at Banff in January 1945 following a mid air collision between Wing Commander Phillips and Flying officer Bonnet. This shows the amount of damage which could be sustained and a safe return made to base. The aircraft was returned to service.**

Service history: Beaufighters were replaced by Mosquito FB.VIs which became operational on 16 June, the role of the squadron being anti-shipping strikes, with two Do217s shot down on 21 July by the CO, Wing Commander J V Yonge. On 12 August a ship was sunk with another damaged, a result which was repeated on the 29th of the month. In September the squadron joined the Banff Strike Wing with Beaufighters of Nos.144 and 404 Squadrons, flying anti-ship and anti-submarine strikes in the Norwegian region. Two ships were set on fire on 14 November, with 18 attacked in December. Although the intensity of operations was reducing, successes were still being achieved with two ships destroyed in February 1945 and two U-boats in March, in addition to a steady score of enemy aircraft. The final operation as part of the Wing was on 31 May and the squadron disbanded on 10 July 1945.

239

SQUADRON

Code Letters:

HB

Usage:
Mosquito NF.II
Dec 1943 - Sept 1944
Mosquito FB.VI
Dec 1943 – Feb 1945
Mosquito NF.30
Jan 1945 – July 1945

Bases:

Ayr 9 – 12.43
West Raynham 12.43 – 7.45

Service history: Following Army Co-operation duties, the squadron moved to Ayr on 30 September 1943 to change to night fighter duties, training on Ansons. A move was made south to West Raynham in December with Mosquito NF.IIs, and the squadron was declared operational in time to fly the first operation on 27 January 1944. In the night fighter role it was part of 100 Group providing fighter support for the night bomber raids. The first claim was a Bf110 on 28 January, but one No.239 Squadron crew was also lost. Initial operations were hampered by the use of early Mosquitos with high unserviceability in both the aircraft and engines, but there was a reluctance to risk the loss of the latest AI radar over enemy territory with the newer Mosquitos. The squadron flew *Serrate* patrols during the day and claims began to increase in April. In June the squadron was providing support to the Allied invasion over the Normandy beach-head, later extending over Northern France as the Allies advanced. By the Autumn the squadron was also flying day *Rangers*, but by the end of the year, the squadron was back to exclusive night fighting, with bomber support continuing until the end of the war. The squadron was disbanded at West Raynham on 1 July 1945.

Above: **No.239 Squadron crew Bailey and White with their groundcrew. The squadron began operations with NF.IIs and FB.VIs in December 1943, later converting to NF.30s.**

Below: **Early NF.IIs were used on the intruder sorties flown early in 1944 in support of Bomber Command because of the possibility that new radar could fall into enemy hands. Unfortunately this often meant old aircraft and engines becoming unservicable.**

248

SQUADRON
Code Letters:
DM

Usage:
Mosquito FB.VI
Dec 1943 - Sept 1946
Mosquito FB.XVIII

Bases:

Predannack 1.43 – 2.44
Portreath 2.44 – 9.44
Banff 9.44 – 7.45
Chivenor 7.45 – 5.46
Thorney Island 5.46 – 9.46

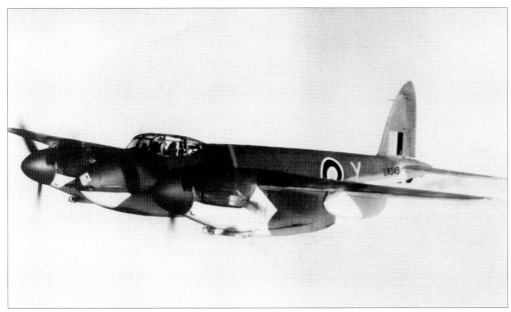

Above: **Squadron Leader Randall, OC 'B' Flight of No.248 Squadron flying Mosquito FB.VI LR349 'Y' from Predannack on 5 January 1944.**

Above: **Squadron Leader Maurice, OC 'A Flight' of No.248 Squadron with other members of the unit.**

Service history: Allocated to the anti-shipping role, No.248 Squadron began to replace their Beaufighters with Mosquitos in December 1943, the last Beaufighter operation being in January 1944. In February Mosquito patrols were started with the first anti-shipping attack on 10 March, escorting Mosquito FB.XVIIIs. The Mosquito XVIIIs were operated by No.618 Squadron aircrew on detachment to No.248 Squadron. Normally the Mk.XVIIIs attacked U-boats or shipping with the FB.VIs providing air cover. Over 100 sorties were being flown monthly, increasing in June to nearly 300 on anti-shipping, anti-submarine and flak suppression. One U-boat was sunk and another damaged during the invasion period and in September the squadron joined the Banff Wing. From here it flew *Rovers* over the Norwegian coastal areas concentrating on anti-submarine patrols. These continued until the Mk.XVIIIs flew their last operation on 15 January 1945, after which the squadron concentrated on anti-shipping patrols with the Mk.VIs. However, the temptation of two surfaced U-boats on 9 April was too great. Using RP one was destroyed and one damaged. In July the squadron moved to experimental strikes on captured enemy U-boats known as *Operation Deadlight*. The squadron remained as one of the few coastal strike units until 1 October 1946, when it was renumbered No.36 Squadron at Thorney Island

Right: **Mosquito FB.XVIIIs were used by No.248 Squadron together with the FB.VIs in combined anti-shipping strikes. The 57mm Molins cannon was particularly effective against surfaced U-boats. Mosquito FB.XVIII NT225 of No.248 Squadron is seen here with invasion stripes in June 1944.**

The Banff Strike Wing

Located in a remote part of Scotland, the Banff Strike Wing replaced its Beaufighters with Mosquito FB.Mk.VIs for use against enemy surface shipping and U-boats along the Norwegian coast, around Denmark and into the Baltic Sea. These Mosquito FB.VIs had the usual armament of four nose mounted fixed 0.303inch machine guns and four under fuselage mounted 20mm cannons, with the addition of up to eight underwing mounted rocket projectiles (RP). The machine guns were effective in assisting the aiming of the combined weapons, the cannons being used to suppress the often damaging gun fire from the well defended targets. One Mosquito could deliver the equivalent of a broadside of guns from a cruiser, a direct hit with RP

disabling most types of coastal shipping. Explosive warhead RP was not used by Mosquitos to avoid the hazard of being blown up by their own weapons as they passed over the target.

The Banff Strike Wing consisted initially of Nos.248, 235 and 333(Norwegian) Squadrons, 248 Squadron having operated from Portreath in Cornwall with Mosquito FB.XVIIIs over the Bay of Biscay against German U-boats using the 6lb 57mm Mollins cannon in place of the normal 20mm cannons. Using the nose mounted 0.303inch machine guns for aiming, the shells from the cannon were fired at the base of the conning tower of the enemy submarine. The wooden Mosquito airframe withstood the recoil shock

Above: **Group Captain Max Aitken, commanding officer of the Banff Strike Wing ready for departure in Mosquito FB.VI HR366 in early 1945.**

Left: **A typical scene at the desolate Banff airfield with ship-busting Mosquito FB.VIs of the Strike Wing taxying past resident No.143 Squadron Mosquitos and a Station Flight Proctor.**

Right: **A Mosquito FB.VI of No.143 Squadron being prepared at Banff. Rocket projectiles are loaded under the wing on four rails on each side while the guns are being cleaned. This work had to be done in all weathers as there were insufficient hangars at Banff to house all the aircraft.**

of the large gun well, and momentarily slowed down when it was fired. No squadron was equipped entirely with Mosquito Mk.XVIIIs, the anti-shipping patrols being flown with a mix of standard FB.Mk.VIs alongside the big gun armed version to provide the widest possible capability against any targets which presented themselves.

The re-equipping of No.248 Squadron began with Mosquitos in December 1943 ready for operations to commence on 20 February 1944. The first major action was on 10 March against an enemy naval force and on D-Day the squadron was allocated the considerable task of protecting Allied shipping from attacks by enemy surface shipping and U-boats. Despite a number of inconclusive attacks on U-boats, the Mk.XVIIIs of No.248 Squadron were finally able to share a claim with a Liberator on U-

821, which was sunk on 10 June. Also in June, No.248 was joined by No.235 Squadron at Portreath, making its first operational sortie on 16 June with Beaufighters, which were replaced by Mosquito FB.VIs by 22 June.

With the retreat of German land forces across Europe, the enemy shipping threat was much reduced in the Bay of Biscay, the last sortie being made on 7 September, before a move to Banff where the two squadrons joined No.333(Norwegian) Squadron to form the Banff Strike Wing. The Mosquitos were mostly used in support of anti-shipping strikes by Beaufighters of Nos.144 and 404 Squadrons. The attacks were mainly along the Norwegian coastline, guided by the Norwegian pilots to pinpoint targets. The reaction had to be rapid if a ship was to be destroyed at anchor before there was time for it to get to

Below: **Four RPs (Rocket Projectiles) mounted under the port wing of a No.143 Squadron Mosquito FB.VI at Banff.**

Below: **Group Captain Max Aitken, son of Lord Beaverbrook, the Minister of Aircraft Production, briefing squadron commanders of the Banff Strike Wing,**

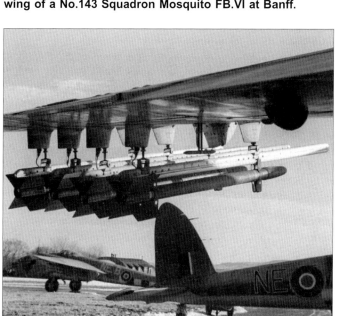

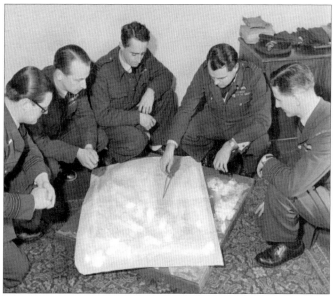

Above: **Mosquito FB.VI HR362, with RPs on underwing rails, of the Banff Strike Wing flying near the Scottish coast.**

sea again, and become a more difficult mobile target. Many of the enemy ships carried heavy armament, with more guns based on the shore around the place of shelter. The Mosquito FB.VIs were particularly effective in countering these defences by keeping enemy heads down during an attack.

The first combined strike from Banff was made on 14 September 1944, when twenty-five Mosquito FB.VIs of Nos.235 and 248 Squadrons, four Mk.XVIIIs of 248 Squadron and nineteen Beaufighters of Nos.144 and 404 Squadrons flew an armed reconnaissance off the Norwe-

gian coast. As a result, four motor vessels and the two escorts were attacked and left burning. On 26 October 60lb(110kg) RPs were fired for the first time, the ideal dive angle being 20 degrees.

With the increase in numbers of Mosquito FB.VIs, No.143 Squadron was formed at Banff to replace some of the Beaufighters. The squadron had previously operated Beaufighters at North Coates, but had never been in action as its role was as an operational training unit (OTU) responsible for working up new crews before they were posted to operational units. The move to join the Banff Wing was therefore greeted with enthusiasm by the crews, as it also meant converting to Mosquitos.

Squadron Leader David Pritchard joined No.143 Squadron at Banff as 'A Flight' Commander, the task being mainly the firing of RPs. The gun sight was depressed by 5 to 6 degrees and aimed at the waterline of the target ship below the funnel. The cannons were fired in a 20 degree dive, and when they struck the bridge the range was 600 yards (548m), the correct distance for firing the RP. Although the RPs could be fired in pairs, they were normally fired in a salvo of eight, harmonised for two dry hits on the superstructure, two on the water line and four to fall short. These four flattened out in the water and

Left: **Close-up of the revised RP launcher configuration on a Banff Strike Wing Mosquito FB.VI.**

Above: **Mosquitos of No.143 Squadron attacking shipping in Sandefjord on 2 April 1945.**

punched through the hull into the engine room. Not only would the ship then start filling with water, but the rocket motors would wreck the boilers and set fire to the oil and fuel pouring out of the fractured pipes in the engine room. As the aircraft flew over the target all appeared quiet, but on looking back when the aircraft had reformed, the ships would either be burning or inverted, soon to disappear below the waves.

Operations commenced by No.143 Squadron on 7 November 1944 not normally carrying bombs, but contributing to the combined attacks of the remainder of the Wing. On 21 November, the largest strike so far was made against shipping in Aalesund. Thirty-two Mosquito fighter-bombers, with No.333 Squadron Mosquitos, plus forty-two Beaufighters and top cover of twelve Mustangs made the attack. On 15 January 1945 an attack was made on well defended shipping in Leirvik harbour and nine experienced FW190 fighter pilots helped to destroy six Mosquitos lost

Right: **When greater range was required, underwing drop tanks were fitted and eight RP were mounted on revised launchers in pairs, one above the other.**

Left: **Squadron Leader David Pritchard flying Mosquito RS625:NE-D of No.143 Squadron on 6 April 1945. It carries underwing fuel tanks and RPs.**

Left: **Led by Squadron Leader David Pritchard, No.143 Squadron Mosquito FB.VIs destroyed three U-boats on 9 May 1945. The RPs can be seen launched in a full salvo of eight photographed from the launch aircraft, while another Mosquito flies over the target surrounded by spray from the hits.**

Left: **Mosquitos of the Banff Strike Wing were returning from a sortie over the Kattegat on 21 April 1945, when they intercepted a force of eighteen German torpedo bombers, shooting down eight of them. The action took place about 150 miles from the Scottish coast. The explosion in the sea is where one of the enemy aircraft fell.**

Above: **An indication of how low the Mosquitos flew during attacks is this strike on shipping along the coast of Norway on 23 March 1945 by the Banff Strike Wing.**

on this raid. One of these losses was David Pritchard's regular aircraft being flown by another crew, which was replaced by RS625 coded NE-D.

The RP installation caused extra drag and was heavy, loaded or unloaded, but there was also a need for extra endurance resulting in fuel drop tanks being hung under the wings which meant removing the inboard pair of RP rails. The loss of punch was overcome by mounting rockets in pairs on modified rails. When faced with combat the tanks were jettisoned, but sometimes broke away sideways wiping off the RP. To avoid this a steel structure was fitted between the RP and fuel tanks, adding more weight and drag.

In March 1945, Mosquitos began to operate without Beaufighters, with shipping the main targets. On some of the larger operations Warwicks of No.279 Squadron were available to drop survival gear to ditched aircrew. While many squadrons in Europe were slackening off operations coastal strike units remained active with a film Mosquito accompanying most raids, in addition to the cameras normally fitted to the strike force, to record success.

On 9 April came the climax to the U-boat search when a force of thirty-seven Mosquitos from Nos.143, 235 and 248 Squadrons was patrolling the Kattegat looking for enemy shipping. David Pritchard was leading 143 Squadron from the rear, with a brief to look for isolated targets by breaking away from the formation. Some wakes of ships

were spotted in the bright afternoon sun and the leader called for a break to investigate. As they turned to port the wingman called that he had spotted U-boats on the surface. The nine aircraft roared in to attack out of the sun at low level, and were not spotted until too late. Hearing the action, the remainder of the wing turned to join in the excitement. The U-boats crash dived, but too late, as one popped up like a cork and exploded violently, sucking down the unfortunate 2nd TAF film Mosquito in the water spout. All three submarines, U-804, U-843 and U-1065 were claimed and confirmed as destroyed. Despite the loss of the film Mosquito, some excellent combat shots were captured on film.

A further German submarine, U-251, was sunk in the Kattegat on 19 April, and four days later a force of forty-five Mosquitos from Banff came across eighteen Junkers torpedo bombers about 150 miles off the Scottish coast on the way to attack Allied shipping. At least nine of the enemy aircraft were destroyed. At a late stage, No.404 Squadron began to convert to Mosquitos from Beaufighters, half the squadron starting training at Banff on 24 March, with the remainder following on 3 April. On their first operation a Bv138 flying boat was destroyed at anchor.

The final shipping strike was made on 4 May against a large well defended convoy near Keil, resulting in a massive battle. A force of forty-eight aircraft was used in the attack, including eight No.404 Squadron Mosquitos which

53

Left: **A low level attack on a pair of U-boats in the Kattegat on 2 May 1945.**

877 BNF 2 MAY 45. /L/143// 6⅜. ATTACK ON 2 U-BOATS KATTEGAT. 57°29′N. 11°24′E

were taking part in their second and last major strike. One aircraft flew so low that the top of a mast complete with German ensign was embedded in the nose. Operations finally ceased on 21 May when Nos.143 and 248 Squadrons supplied two Mosquitos each for an anti U-boat patrol, but found only E-boats.

The Mosquito FB.VI, the most common variant of the Mosquito family, more than justified its existence carrying ever increasing war loads and was a difficult target for navy gunners to hit. Ernst Heinkel, the famous German aircraft designer once said of the Mosquito; "That is the aircraft I would like to have designed" and after the war kept a picture of the Mosquito in pride of place in his board room.

Left: **Low over the target U-boats with two other Mosquitos climbing away before returning to Banff.**

Left: **An attack by a Mosquito of No.143 Squadron on enemy shipping on 4 May 1945.**

249
SQUADRON
Code Letters:
GN

Usage:
Mosquito FB.Mk.26
Mar 1946 - Aug 1946

Bases:

Eastleigh, Kenya 3.46 – 6.46
Habbaniya, Iraq 6.46 – 9.46

Right: **Mosquito T.III RR289 of No.249 Squadron** stored at 107 MU, Kasfareet in Egypt in 1947 was withdrawn from use due to the separation of glue joints. The Mosquitos were withdrawn on 28 August and the squadron converted to Tempests.

Left and below: **Mosquito FB.XVIII PZ468 QM-D of No.254 Squadron.** The squadron was equipped with Beaufighters but with the war nearly over it received some Mosquito FB.VIs and FB.XVIIIs with the 57mm Molins cannon for anti-submarine operations. On 4 May a large enemy ship and a destroyer were sunk by the squadron. This was followed by an attack on three U-boats, in which one was sunk and another damaged.
The last operation by the squadron was an ASR search on 11 May. The Mosquitos were withdrawn leaving the torpedo Beaufighters until it was renumbered No.42 Squadron.

254
SQUADRON
Code Letters:
QM

Usage:
Mosquito FB.VI/XVIII
Apr 1945 - Nov 1945

Bases:

North Coates 11.42 – 6.45
Chivenor 6 – 11.45

255

SQUADRON
Code Letters:
YD

Usage:
Mosquito NF.XIX
Jan 1945 - 1945
Mosquito NF.30
Apr 1945 – Arp 1946

Bases:

Foggia Main, Italy 1.44 – 2.45
Rosignano 2.45 – 9.45
Hal Far 9.45 – 1.46
Gianaclis 1.46 – 4.46

Above: **No.255 Squadron operated Mosquito NF.XIX and NF.30s from February 1945. The first Mosquitos arrived with the squadron in January 1945, starting the replacement of Beaufighters. The first Mosquito operation was on 26 February with the squadron responsible for the night defence of all Italy. To cover the entire country a number of detachments were made, with random patrols being flown resulting in three combats during 1945. In September the squadron retired to Hal Far, and moved to Giannaclis in January 1946 where it was disbanded 30 April 1946.**

Service history: In May 1943 No.256 Squadron began to convert to Mosquitos from Beaufighters with the first success claimed on 11 June. The squadron also operated Malta detachments from July and by the 18th twelve enemy aircraft had been claimed as night successes. In October, the entire squadron joined the detachment and shared its duties between the night defence of Malta and nocturnal convoy patrols. In February 1944 there was a detachment to Alghero to begin intruder operations over Italy, which lasted until the end of March. In July, intruder operations started over France, returning to Italy from September onwards. A detachment returned to Malta in February 1945 as night defence of the Yalta conference between the Allied leaders. In March, the squadron was intruding over the Balkans with some Mosquito FB.VIs to deliver bombs, with intense operations until the end of the war. It was equipped with Mk.VIs entirely, but returned to the night fighter role in October. By May 1946, the squadron had reduced to one flight only, also flying Mosquito PR.XVIs for weather operations until being disbanded on 12 September 1946.

Below: **TA407 'O' with No.256 Squadron.**

256

SQUADRON
Code Letters:
JT

Usage:
Mosquito NF.XII
May 1943 – July 1944
Feb - May 1945
Mosquito NF.XIII
Jan 1944 – May 1945
Mosquito FB.VI
Apr 1945 – May 1945
June 1945 – Oct 1945

Bases:

Ford 4.43 – 8.43
Woodvale 8.43 – 9.43
Malta 9.43 – 10.43
Luqa 10.43 – 4.44
La Senia, Italy 4.43 – 9.44
Foggia 9.44 – 2.45
Forli 2.45 – 8.45
to Egypt 8.45 –9.45
El Ballah 9.45 – 12.45
Deversoir 12.45 – 7.46
Nicosia 7.46 – 9.46

264

SQUADRON
Code Letters:

PS

Usage:
Mosquito NF.II
May 1942 – Jan 1944
Mosquito FB.IV
Aug 1943 – Oct 1943
Mosquito NF.XIII
Dec 1943 – Aug 1945
Mosquito NF.36
Nov 1945 – Dec 1951

Bases:

Colerne 5.41 – 4.43
Predannack 4.43 – 7.43
Fairwood Common
7.43 – 11.43
Coleby Grange 11.43 – 12.43
Church Fenton 12.43 – 5.44
Blackbushe 5.44 – 7.44
Hunsdon 7.44 – 8.44
France 8.44 – 9.44
Predannack 9.44 – 11.44
Colerne 11.44 – 12.44
Odiham 12.44 – 1.45
Lille 1.45 – 4.45
Gilze Rijen 4.45 – 5.45
Rheine 5.45 – 6.45
Twente 6.45 – 8.45
Church Fenton 11.45 – 1946
Wittering 1946 – 1.48
Coltishall 1.48 – 11.49
Church Fenton 9.50 – 8.51
Linton-on-Ouse 8.51 – 12.51

Above: **A pair of Mosquito F.Mk.IIs of No.264 Squadron fly over Colerne in April 1943. In May 1942, the first Mosquito NF.II arrived with the squadron to begin the replacement of Defiants, becoming operational by 8 June. In December the squadron began day patrols over the Bay of Biscay, flying shipping reconnaissance patrols over the Western Approaches. The level of operations began to increase and on 20 June a BV138 was destroyed and a Ju88 claimed as a probable.**

Below: **Mosquito F.Mk.II intruders of No.264 Squadron at Colerne in April 1943.**

Above: **No.264 Squadron aircrew by a Mosquito F.II at Predannack in 1943.**

Above: **Squadron Leader Michael Constable-Maxwell (on wing) and his navigator Flight Lieutenant John Quinton of No.264 Squadron at Colerne who completed three tours together. On 13 August 1951, Quinton gave his parachute to an ATC cadet when his 228 OCU Wellington collided with another aircraft and crashed following loss of control.**

Left: **This No.264 Squadron Mosquito NF.XIII landed safely in Normandy in August 1944 after being damaged by debris from an enemy raider. (DHAHC collection)**

In 1944, the older Mosquitos were replaced by Mosquito NF.XIIIs with improved Mk.VIII AI radar. In May, the squadron moved south to cover the planned Allied invasion. Following the landings in France, the squadron began beach-head patrols in support of the ground forces, and on 10 June, claimed its 100th victory.

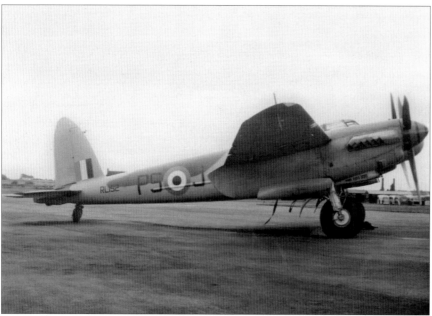

In July and August 1944 the squadron was used for anti-diver defence and was one of the few night-fighter units to operate from the beach-head, flying with the 2nd TAF until September, when a return was made to the Western Approaches. At the end of 1944 the squadron returned to the 2nd TAF, patrolling the advancing front line and up to 450 miles from its base. With the end of the war the squadron ran down, and was disbanded at Twente on 25 August 1945. On 20 November 1945, No.125 Squadron was renumbered No.264 Squadron as part of 12 Group, Fighter Command, equipped with Mosquito NF.36s, re-equipping with Meteor NF.11s in December 1951.

Left: **Mosquito NF.36 RL152 PS-J of No.264 Squadron at Acklington in 1951. (DHAHC collection).**

268
SQUADRON

Usage:
Mosquito FB.IV
Sept 1945 – Mar 1946

Bases:

Cambrai, France 9.45 – 3.46

Above: **No.268 Squadron operated Mosquito FB.VIs in the light bomber role in France using aircraft similar to HJ716. The squadron officially became No.268(B) Squadron on 19 September 1945 when 487(B) Squadron was renumbered, and based in France as part of BAFO operating as a light bomber unit. The squadron was disbanded on 31 March 1946.**

Right: **Mosquito FB.VI of No.305 Squadron with underwing bombs at Lasham when the unit was part of the 2nd TAF. (J B Cynk)**

305
(Polish)
SQUADRON

Code Letters:
SM

Usage:
Mosquito FB.IV
Dec 1943 – Nov 1946

Bases:

Lasham 11.43 – 10.44
Blackbushe 10.44
Lasham 10.44
Blackbushe 10.44 – 11.44
Cambrai 11.44 – 7.45
Volkel 7.45 – 9.45
Gilze Rijen 9.45 – 11.45
Brussels 11.45 – 3.46
Wahn 3.46 – 10.46
Faldingworth 10.46 – 1.47

Service history: As part of 138 Wing 2nd TAF with Nos.107 and 613 Squadrons, the Mitchells were replaced by Mosquitos from December 1943, the role being a combination of light bomber and fighter intruder duties. Operations were during the day and night and two of the most notable attacks were the bombing of the enemy sabotage school at Chateau Maulny on 2 August 1944, and the destruction of a few millions of gallons of fuel near Nancy on 31 August. The destruction of the fuel deprived the enemy tanks and aircraft of petrol during the vital Battle of Normandy. Following the end of the war, No.305 Squadron became part of British Forces of Occupation (BAFO) until November 1946 when it was transferred back to the UK. The Mosquitos were withdrawn by 25 November 1946, and the squadron formally disbanded on 6 January 1947.

307

(Polish)
SQUADRON

Code Letters:
EW

Usage:
Mosquito NF.II
Jan 1943 – 1944
Mosquito FB.VI
Sept 1943 – Oct 1943
Mosquito NF.XII
Feb 1944 – Nov 1944
Mosquito NF.30
Oct 1944 – Jan 1947

Bases:

Exeter 4.41 – 4.43
Fairwood Common
4.43 – 8.43
Predannack 8.43 – 11.43
Drem 11.43 – 3.44
Coleby Grange 3.44 – 5.44
Church Fenton 5.44 – 1.45
Castle Camps 1.45 – 5.45
Coltishall 5.45 – 8.45
Horsham St Faith 8.45 – 1.47

Above: **Mosquito NF.II trainer of No.307 (Lwowski) Squadron fitted with AI Mk.V, but no guns during conversion to the Mosquito at Exeter in September 1942. (J B Cynk)**

Right: **Ground crew of No.307 Squadron prepare to start a Mosquito NF.Mk.30 at Castle Camps in January 1945.**
(J B Cynk)

Below: **The crew board a No.307 Squadron Mosquito NF.30 at Castle Camps on 27 January 1945. (J B Cynk)**

Service history: In the New Year of 1943 the squadron began to replace Beaufighters with Mosquito NF.IIs while remaining operational, the first Mosquito action being on 15 February. The squadron was on the offensive by May, flying *Rangers*, and in June began daylight *Instep* patrols. In November a move was made to Drem for shipping patrols, but with the approach of the second front, the squadron returned south to fly night intruders over Europe. In September the squadron joined in anti-diver patrols, but there was little success at night against V.1s. In December a return was made to intruding with the addition of bomber support reaching nearly 300 night operational hours per month. With the end of fighting in Europe, the squadron remained in Fighter Command as part of the peacetime night defence of the UK until disbanding at Horsham St Faith on 2 January 1947.

333

(Norwegian)
SQUADRON
Code Letters:
KK

Usage:
Mosquito NF.II
Oct 1943 – 1944
Mosquito FB.VI
Oct 1943 – Nov 1944

Bases:

*Leuchars & Woodhaven
10.43 – 9.44
Banff 9.44 – 11.45*

Above: **Mosquito F.II DZ700 'H' of No.333 (Norwegian) Squadron 'B Flight' at Banff.**

Service history: On 10 May 1943 No.1477 (Norwegian) Flight was expanded to a full squadron strength as No.333 Squadron with dual roles. Mosquitos were based at Leuchars and Catalinas at Woodhaven, both parts flying convoy and shipping support, and anti-submarine patrols over the North Sea and the Norwegian coastline. A number of enemy aircraft were claimed by the squadron and, in 1944, U-boats became primary targets with the Mosquitos carrying depth charges. In June one U-boat was sunk for the loss of two Mosquitos, and in September the squadron became part of the Banff Strike Wing with an increased level of activity. Mines were dropped by Mosquitos in the Norwegian fjords and maritime navigational aids were destroyed to disrupt enemy shipping. With the end of hostilities the squadron was transferred to the Royal Norwegian Air Force on 21 November 1945.

Below: **Mosquito NF.IIs of No.333 Squadron 'B Flight' at Banff: DZ754 'F' in the background.**

404

(RCAF)
SQUADRON

Code Letters:

EO

Usage:
Mosquito FB.IV
Mar 1945 – May 1945

Bases:

Banff 3.45 – 5.45

Above: **No.404 Squadron began to convert from Beaufighters to Mosquitos in March 1945 as part of the Banff Strike Wing, sending out 47 sorties before the war ended. The squadron was disbanded at Banff on 25 May 1945.**

Service history: The squadron started to convert from Beaufighters in April 1944 and completed by August, the duties including defence of the troops and equipment being built up for the Allied invasion of Europe. By this time the earlier Mosquitos were obsolete, but by August they had been replaced by the more effective NF.30s. These new aircraft were used for intensive intruder operations from Manston in December, providing standing fighter patrols over enemy fighter airfields while bomber raids were in progress. Long range night *Rangers* were also flown with the CO, Wing Commander Russ Bannock DFC claiming the first victory on Christmas Eve 1944. The total of wartime victories claimed by the squadron in four months of operations was 23 aircraft in the air and ten on the ground. With the war over the squadron moved to Predannack, where it was disbanded on 1 September 1945.

Below: **Squadron Leader MacFadyen's Mosquito NF.30 of No.406 Squadron RCAF. (Public Archives of Canada)**

406

(RCAF)
SQUADRON

Code Letters:

HU

Usage:
Mosquito NF.XII
Apr 1944 – July 1944
Mosquito NF.30
July 1944 – Sept 1945

Bases:

Winkleigh 4.44 – 9.44
Colerne 9.44 – 11.44
Manston 11.44 – 7.45
Predannack 7.45 – 9.45

Above: **Mosquito NF.XIII MM466 of 409 (RCAF) Squadron dispersed on a wintry European airfield on 31 January 1945.**

409

(RCAF)
SQUADRON
Code Letters:

KP

Usage:
Mosquito NF.XIII
Mar 1944 – July 1945

Bases:

Acklington 2.43 – 5.44
West Malling 5.44 – 1944
Hunsdon 1944 – 8.44
France 8.44 – 4.45
Rheine 4.45 – 5.45
Holland 5.45 – 7.45

Left: **Wing Commander P Y Davoud, CO of No.409 (Nighthawk) Squadron with his dog *Beau* and a damaged enemy propeller blade, used as a score board by the unit at Coleby Grange in November 1942. (Public Archives of Canada)**

Below: **Mosquito NF.XIII MM512 of No.409 (RCAF) Squadron at the recaptured Carpiquet airfield in France on 26 August 1944. (Photo Archives of Canada)**

Service history: In March 1944 the squadron converted from Beaufighters to Mosquitos and also transferred into 85 Group as part of the 2nd TAF. Training began on intruding and night-cover patrols with the squadron returning to the offensive in time for the D-Day landings. The main initial duty was to fly over the beach-head, making the first claim of a Ju188 on 9 June, the score reaching 11 enemy aircraft by the end of the month. The squadron was also tasked with anti-diver patrols until the middle of July when the squadron returned to intruding over occupied Europe making a number of claims. No.409 Squadron was the first night fighter unit to be based in France, moving forward with the advancing Allied armies until reaching Germany. During one night in April the squadron claimed six enemy aircraft in one night, three by one crew – Flying Officer E E Hermanson and Flight Lieutenant D J I Hamm. The following night, on the squadron's last action, three more enemy aircraft were claimed. With the war over in Europe the squadron moved to Holland and was disbanded at Twente on 1 July 1945.

410

(RCAF)
SQUADRON
Code Letters:
RA

Usage:
Mosquito NF.II
Oct 1942 – Dec 1943
Mosquito FB.VI
July 1943 – Sept 1943
Mosquito NF.XIII
Dec 1943 – Aug 1944
Mosquito NF.30
Aug 1944 – June 1945

Bases:

Acklington 10.42 – 2.43
Coleby Grange 2.43 – 10.43
West Malling 10.43 – 11.43
Hunsdon 11.43 – 12.43
Castle Camps 12.43 – 4.44
Hunsdon 4.44 – 6.44
Zeals 6.44 – 7.44
Colerne 7.44 – 9.44
Hunsdon 9.44
France 9.44 – 4.45
Gilze-Rijen 4.45 – 6.45

Above: **Flight Lieutenant M A Cybulski (left) and Flying Officer H H Ladbrook with their charred Mosquito NF.II DZ757 RA-Q at Coleby Grange. They had destroyed a Do217 on 27 September 1944 and flew through the burning wreckage; each was awarded the DFC.**

Right: **Mosquito NF.II DZ726 RA-Z of No.410 (RCAF) Squadron with Wing Commander F W Hillock (left) and Flight Lieutenant P O'Neill-Dunne holding 300 feet of copper cable brought home from a low level sortie to Apeldoorn on 15 April 1943.**

Service history: Having operated Defiants and Beaufighters in the night fighter role since June 1941, the squadron commenced converting to Mosquito NF.IIs in October 1942 and completed by 26 January 1943. In February the squadron moved south to relieve No.409 Squadron on night *Rangers*, followed by bomber support operations. In October the squadron joined 11 Group as a night fighter unit, receiving NF.XIIIs equipped with AI Mk.VIII. After the D-Day landings, the squadron provided beach head support patrols at night, followed by the gradual conversion to NF.30s, when the squadron joined the 2nd TAF. The squadron continued to claim successes against enemy aircraft throughout the winter, with the eventual claims by the unit of 75 ¾ destroyed, two probables and eight damaged. Disbandment came at Gilze-Rijen on 9 June 1945.

Below: **Mosquito NF.XIII HK429 RA-N of No.410 (RCAF) Squadron in which Flying Officer E Hermanson and Flight Lieutenant D Hamm scored a triple victory on the night of 23/24 April 1945 while operating over Europe.**

Above: **Mosquito FB.VI HR147 TH-Z "Hairless Joe" flown by Wing Commander Russ Bannock DSO, DFC with a scoreboard of eight enemy aircraft and 19 V.1s. Russ Bannock became the top-scoring pilot against V.1s, claiming a total of 18.5 destroyed.**

Left: **The crews of No.418 (RCAF) Squadron decorated their Mosquitos with art-work, names and scores. "Cousin Jake" has a score of 32 enemy aircraft and two V.1s**

Below: **Crews of No.418 (RCAF) Squadron prepare for the next Intruder sortie while based at Ford.**

Service history: In March 1943 the squadron moved south to replace its Bostons with Mosquito FB.VIs. In September three crews were attached to No.617 Squadron for bomber escort duties and day *Rangers* started in November, continuing into the New Year. Flying round the clock from February 1944 the success rate increased with the 100th victory on 2 May. The squadron continued intruding during the Allied invasion of Europe until being allocated to night anti-diver patrols. A return was made to *Rangers* and *Big Ben* operations against V.2 launch sites from September, but the squadron was transferred from 11 Group to 2 Group 2nd TAF in the light bomber role on 21 November 1944. A move was made the same day from Hunsdon to Blackbushe where the squadron went on close support operations until it was disbanded at Volkel on 7 September 1945.

456

(RAAF) SQUADRON

Code Letters:

RX

Usage:
Mosquito NF.II
Dec 1942 – Feb 1944
Mosquito FB.VI
July 1943 – Feb 1944
Mosquito NF.XVII
Jan 1944 – Dec 1944
Mosquito NF.30
Dec 1944 – June 1945

Bases:

Valley 6.41 – 3.43
Middle Wallop 3.43 - 10.43
Colerne 10.43 – 11.43
Fairwood Common
11.43 – 2.44
Ford 2.44 – 12.44
Church Fenton 12.44 – 3.45
Bradwell Bay 3.45 – 6.45

Above: **Mosquito NF.Mk.II DZ681 of No.456 (RAAF) Squadron at dispersal.**

Right: **Leavesden built Mosquito NF.30 NT264/G RX-R operating from Valley,** although normally based at Church Fenton. The G after the serial indicates the classified nature of this aircraft - requiring constant guarding when on the ground.

Below: **Mosquito NF.30 of No.456 (RAAF) Squadron in a blister hangar at Church Fenton during maintenance.**

Service history: No.456, the RAAF's night fighter squadron, was formed at Valley with Defiants on 30 June 1941, re-equipping with Mosquito NF.IIs from 30 December 1942 when the first three arrived. At the end of February 1942, in addition to the night fighter role, day *Rangers* and day fighter operations were undertaken. The Intruder operations included destroying the French railway system by day and French airfields at night. Later in the summer the *Ranger* operations included attacks on power stations, and a specific *Ranger* flight was formed with FB.VIs adding *Instep* patrols against shipping over the Bay of Biscay. The squadron re-equipped with later Mosquitos from January 1944 ready for the night defence of southern Britain during the build-up for D-Day. With the V.1 menace, the squadron was put on anti-diver patrols as well as providing night cover over France. At the end of the year the squadron converted to NF.30s and the unit was active against enemy fighters over RAF bomber airfields. In March a detachment at Bradwell Bay was allocated to bomber support duties, later joined by the rest of the squadron until the end of the war. The squadron was disbanded at Bradwell Bay on 15 June 1945.

Above: **No.464 Squadron Mosquito FB.VIs at Hatfield on 2 June 1944. (DH Photo)**

464

(RAAF)
SQUADRON
Code Letters:

SB

Usage:
Mosquito F.VI
Aug 1943 – Sept 1945

Bases:

Sculthorpe 7.43 – 12.43
Hunsdon 12.43 – 4.44
Gravesend 4.44 – 6.44
Thorney Island 6.44 – 2.45
France 2.45 – 4.45
Brussels 4.45 – 9.45

Right: **Mosquito FB.VI HX977 is serviced at Hunsdon between sorties. (DH Photo)**

Service history: Towards the end of 1943 No.464 Squadron began to convert to Mosquito FB.VIs from Venturas as part of the 2nd TAF. Operations were resumed on 30 October, operating a mix of light bomber and fighter intruder duties by both day and night. The squadron's most notable raid was on the Amiens Prison on 18 February 1944, led by Group Captain P C Pickard and shared with Nos.487 (RNZAF) and 21 Squadrons. Further precision raids undertaken by the same three units were on Gestapo HQs at Aarhus on 31 October 1944 and Copenhagen on 21 March 1945. The squadron finally disbanded on 25 September 1945.

Right: **Mosquito FB.VI MM401 suffered combat damage on 21 February 1944, and on landing back at Hunsdon had the port undercarriage collapse. It is here supported in the snow ready for repairs.**

67

Left: **Corporal N L Kingston checks the Merlin engine on a No.464 Squadron Mosquito at Hunsdon. (DH Photo)**

Left: **Squadron Leader T McPhee (right) and Flight Lieutenant G W Atkins debriefing after their 74th sortie together.**

Below: **Mosquito FB.VIs of No.464 Squadron at Thorney Island in 1944. For some reason the wartime censor has seen a need to crudely blank out the fin leading edges.**

Operation Jericho

The Amiens Prison Raid

In the Somme area and the plains of Picardy, as in most other parts of occupied Europe, there was an active resistance supported by manpower and equipment supplied by the Allies. Led by a formidable trio, the brothers Dominique and Pierre Penchardier and an ex communist known as Pepe, the Amiens area was administered efficiently and secretly. However, the less wary were exposed by traitors and imprisoned in the forbidding Amiens prison. Some had been caught in the act of sabotage, while others had been betrayed by collaborators, and the persuasive methods used by the *Gestapo* put the entire operation at risk. One particularly effective member was twenty year old Jean Beaurin, who had caused five major train crashes, killing and injuring many hundreds of German troops. He was caught and imprisoned at Amiens towards the end of 1943.

By December 1943 twelve members of the resistance organisation had already been shot in the prison, and Beaurin was waiting the same fate with others and little chance of rescue. Then another senior member of the team was caught with a half map of the prison in his possession while planning a rescue attempt, thus alerting the Germans. The final blow was the arrest of Maurice

Above: **Mosquito FB.VI MM417 EG-T of No.487 Squadron as used on the Amiens Prison raid.**

Right: **The model of the Amiens Prison used to brief the crews before departure from Hunsdon. The main prison building was in a cruciform shape alongside a main road with the guard accommodation in a separate building, and the mess attached on the left hand end of the main building.**

Holleville, who was caught trying to acquire ration cards. So clandestine was the organisation that according to the authorities the men did not exist, and were therefore unable to qualify for such essential items as ration cards for food. The leaders of the organisation had pledged to help each other, even if it cost them their lives, but a surface attack on the prison would stand little chance of success, effectively wiping out the already infiltrated network. Then it was heard that their colleagues and about 100 others were due to be shot on 19 February 1944.

Meanwhile, Dominique Penchard began to send details of the Amiens prison to London without giving any reasons, providing precise details of the layout, structure, defences and duty rostas. Fortunately for the resistance, the priority changed when two Allied intelligence officers were captured and joined the inmates of the prison. The moment

Right: **Squadron Leader A McRitchie DFC and his navigator Flight Lieutenant R Sampson of No.464 Squadron at Hunsdon before departure on the Amiens Prison raid on 18 February 1944. They were flying Mosquito FB.VI MM404, SB-T, which was shot down on the raid killing Sampson and wounding Ritchie, who was taken prisoner.**

had come to request a precision air attack on the prison and the task was allocated to the 2nd Tactical Air Force with AVM Basil Embry responsible for the planning. There were about 700 prisoners overall and losses amongst them were inevitable, but many were to be shot anyway and it would give a chance for a number to escape.

The prison was surrounded by high walls and located alongside a long-straight road with no nearby obstructions. The guards were located in a separate building attached to the main cruciform layout prison building. They ate in an adjacent block, making lunchtime the best time to eliminate the maximum number of guards. The balance of weapons used had to be very carefully planned as, when hitting the main prison walls, the explosion had to be enough to breach them and spring the doors without destroying the building. Not only did the guard's mess hall have to be destroyed, but breaches had to be made in the outer walls to allow the prisoners to escape into the surrounding countryside.

No.140 Wing based at Hunsdon was selected to undertake this precision raid using Mosquito FB.VIs. The Wing consisted of Nos.464(RAAF), 487(RNZAF) and 21(RAF) Squadrons. The Wing Leader was Group Captain P C (Percy) Pickard, who was inexperienced in low level attack and undertook ten hours conversion training at Hatfield. The overall raid was to be lead by AVM Basil Embry with Percy Pickard as number two and the attack was ready to go from 10 February. Close support for the raid was to be provided by Typhoons of No.198 Squadron. No.487 Squadron was tasked with bombing the guard's mess and making two breaches in the outer walls, while 464 Squadron was to place its bombs against the main prison walls.

If no prisoners were seen to escape, No.21 Squadron was tasked with the horrifying alternative of bombing the prison and all those in it, as requested by the inmates who were aware of the plan.

The first set-back was that Basil Embry was forbidden to fly on such a hazardous mission, as he was very much involved in the planning for the Allied invasion of Europe. Percy Pickard took over the lead even though he had only the experience of six previous low-level sorties, all against V-1 launch sites. Despite being ready, the weather was

Right: **Group Captain 'Percy' Pickard, left, and his navigator Flight Lieutenant Bill Broadley prepare for departure on the Amiens Prison raid on 18 February 1944, from which they did not return.**

Left: **A low level view of the Amiens Prison during the attack on 18 February 1944, with the guard's mess hall destroyed and bomb damage to the enemy accommodation.**

abysmal, becoming worse after 10 February. There was low cloud and snow across Europe, even the training was hazardous with some aircraft sustaining damage. An expected improvement did not materialise on 14 February and time was running out. With the arrival of 18 February further delay was out of the question and the eighteen Mosquitos, plus a film aircraft, were prepared for departure. The briefing commenced at 08.00hrs under tight security when a model of the prison layout was unveiled revealing the target for the first time to the crews. Surprise and accuracy were essential for success and Group Captain

Pickard was to be at the rear of the second wave to assess the damage and, if required, call in No.21 Squadron. In case anything happened to Pickard and his navigator Alan Broadley, the crew of the Film Unit Mosquito, were to assess the situation and advise No.21 Squadron.

With no improvement in the weather at Hunsdon, but a prospect of improved conditions over the Channel and the target, Pickard made the decision to go only two hours from the deadline for hitting the target, as any delay would have been pointless. The Mosquitos took off into the gloom from Hunsdon's humped runway into weather conditions

Below: **Taken by the Film Unit Mosquito just after the raid, prisoners can be seen escaping from a breach in the outer walls of the Amiens Prison. Damage to the main prison building is considerable, resulting in the regrettable death of some of the prisoners before they could escape.**

Left: **A post raid reconnaissance photo of the Amiens Prison showing the damage, including breaches in the front and rear outer walls.**

which many of the crews had not previously experienced. As a result four aircraft lost contact with the formation and had to find their way back home. However, as had been hoped, a break was found in the cloud over the Channel making the operation possible. Another Mosquito returned due to engine trouble, leaving nine aircraft in the main attack and four in reserve.

At noon the local resistance workers were walking unobtrusively outside the prison to help the escaping prisoners, as they had been doing for a number of days. At one minute past the hour aircraft appeared through the murk, coming in low. Three of No.487 Squadron's Mosquitos aimed for the prison dropping their eleven second delay bombs, while the remaining two made a diversionary fake attacks on the local railway station, before coming back over the prison. The outer walls were breached successfully, but No.464 Squadron was too close behind and had to orbit while the initial bombs went off. A direct hit on the guard house killed or disabled the occupants and as expected a number of the prisoners were killed or wounded, while many were able to escape. Dr Mans and his helpers struggled to help the wounded and released trapped prisoners, even giving medical help to injured Germans. For their heroic acts, many of them were to die later in front of firing squads.

Pickard circled over the prison at 500 feet, watching the escaping figures in the snow, with the Film Unit Mosquito flying just above the prison. Having seen that the operation was a success, Pickard signalled No.21 Squadron to return home. This was his last contact. As he turned for home another Mosquito made a high speed crash landing in open country. The navigator was already dead, but the pilot survived and was made a prisoner of war. Pickard's aircraft was then attacked by an FW190, its fire cutting through the rear fuselage, severing the tail. With total loss of control the Mosquito (HX922:EG-F) crashed, killing the crew instantly and burst into flames.

The final count of prison occupants killed amounted to 87, of which many were Germans. 182 prisoners were recaptured, but 255, half of whom had been waiting execution, managed to escape. The spoof attack on the railway station delayed the occupying troops by two hours and with them came the *Gestapo*. During the month of April some 260 survivors, including those arrested helping in the escape, were shot and buried in a defence ditch at Arras, their bodies not being located until the autumn.

The cost in human lives of this raid was therefore high, but the precision attack by the Mosquitos of 140 Wing proved clearly that such an attack was possible. It was also important for morale, both for the Allies and the French Resistance workers.

Below: **The graves of Pickard and Broadley being tended at Amiens cemetery in 1945.**

Above: **No.487 (RNZAF) Squadron Mosquito FB.VIs from Sculthorpe led by MM417:EG-T.**

487

(RNZAF)
SQUADRON

Code Letters:

EG

Usage:
Mosquito FB.VI
Aug 1943 – Sept 1945

Bases:

Sculthorpe 7.43 – 12.43
Hunsdon 12.43 – 4.44
Gravesend 4.44 – 6.44
Thorney Island 6.44 – 2.45
France 2.45 –4.45
Brussels 4.45 – 7.45
Cambrai 7.45 – 9.45

Left: **Mosquito FB.VI MM417 EG-T again, this time carrying underwing 500lb bombs.**

Below: **Mosquito FB.VI HX917 EG-E of No.487 Squadron taxies from dispersal over the grass at Swanton Morley.**

Service history: On 1 June 1943 No.487 Squadron transferred from Bomber Command to the 2nd TAF in the same Wing as Nos.464 and 21 Squadrons. From August 1943 Mosquito FB.VIs began to replace Venturas, the squadron being mainly employed on night bombing duties as well as daylight precision raids on the Amiens Prison and *Gestapo* HQs at Aarhus University and the Shellhaus building in Copenhagen. At the end of the war, the squadron was renumbered No.16 Squadron in October 1945, later changed to No.268 retrospectively from 19 September.

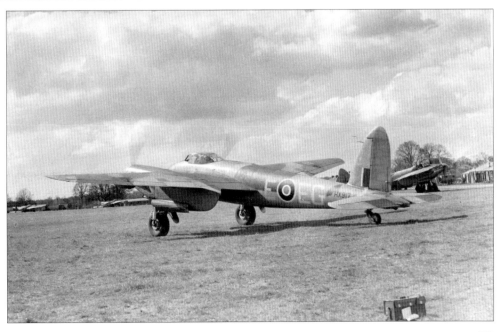

488

(RNZAF) SQUADRON

Code Letters:
ME

Usage:
Mosquito NF.XII
Aug 1943 – May 1944
Mosquito NF.XIII
Oct 1943 – Oct 1944
Mosquito NF.30
Oct 1944 – Apr 1945

Bases:

Drem 8.43 – 9.43
Bradwell Bay 9.43 – 5.44
Zeals 5.44 – 7.44
Colerne 7.44 – 10.44
Hunsdon 10.44 – 11.44
Amiens 11.44 – 4.45
Gilze-Rijen 4.45

Above: **No.488 Squadron was involved in the night defence of Great Britain until moving to France in support of the invading Allied armies in November 1944. NT370 crashed on landing on 27 March 1945.**

Right: **489 Squadron operated Mosquito FB.VIs for less than two months in 1945 at Banff.**

Below: **489 Squadron replaced its Beaufighters with Mosquito FB.VIs in June 1945, but was disbanded before becoming operational on the new type.**

489

SQUADRON
Code Letters:
P6

Usage:
Mosquito FB.VI
June 1945 – Aug 1945

Bases:

Banff 6.45 – 8.45

500 (RAuxAF) SQUADRON

Usage:
Mosquito NF.30
Nov 1946 – 1948

Bases:

West Malling 4.46 – 1957

502 (RAuxAF) SQUADRON

Code Letters:

RAC

Usage:
Mosquito NF.30
Dec 1947 – 1948

Bases:

Aldergrove 12.47 – 1957

504 (RAuxAF) SQUADRON

Code Letters:

RAD

Usage:
Mosquito NF.30
1947 – 1948

Bases:

Hucknall 11.46 – 4.49

500 Squadron (RAuxAF)
Service history: The squadron reformed at West Malling in the night fighter role equipped with Mosquito NF.30s similar to the regular units based there at the time. However, in 1948 Air Ministry policy was for all RAuxAF units to be in the day fighter role. 500 Squadron then became the first Auxiliary unit to convert to Meteor F.3s by the end of the year.

502 Squadron (RAuxAF)
Service history: In December 1947, when the light bomber role was abandoned by the RAuxAF, the squadron converted from Mosquito B.25s to NF.30s in the night fighter role. It had hardly a chance to get started when the policy changed again and the squadron moved to the day fighter role with Spitfires.

504 Squadron (RAuxAF)
Service history: The squadron was formed as a light bomber unit at Hucknall in May 1946, but before it could get started it changed to the night fighter role in 1947. However, this only continued for a year before the role changed again to day fighter with Spitfires.

These squadrons all operated Mosquito NF.30s for a short period after the war, but reverted to the day fighter role due to a change of RAF policy. NF.30 RK953 is a typical example.

515

SQUADRON
Code Letters:
P3

Usage:
Mosquito NF.II
Feb 1944 – 1944
Mosquito FB.VI
Mar 1944 – June 1945

Bases:

Little Snoring 12.43 – 6.45

Above: **Mosquito FB.VI NS993 P3-T of No.515 Squadron which made a successful forced landing in Switzerland on 20 September 1944. This aircraft accompanied PZ440 on a raid to Holykirchen airfield near Munich – see intruder chapter. (DHAHC collection)**

Service history: As part of 100 Group Bomber Command, the squadron was allocated to the bomber support role, replacing Beaufighters from February 1944. Operations started again from 12 March including intruder patrols over enemy occupied French airfields at night, and a specialist role of escorting at night Mosquitos mining the Kiel Canal at low level. The squadron flew day *Rangers* in support of the Allied invasion claiming five successes in the month of June. By August the squadron was principally back to intruding against road and rail targets. In November the first ASH radar equipped Mosquitos were issued to the squadron and following training Squadron Leader C V Bennett claimed a Ju88 on 31 December. Intruder operations continued in 1945 with the final operation on 2 May, followed by disbandment on 10 June 1945.

Below: **Mosquito FB.VI PZ338 of No.515 Squadron at Little Snoring on 4 November 1944 with L to R: Wing Commander F F Lambert DSO, DFC the CO, Squadron Leader Farrell, Flying Officer Lake DFC, AFC and Pilot Officer Groves DFC.**

Intruders

Mosquito Intruder operations bridged the gap between day fighters and fighter-bombers. These operations commenced using standard Mosquito F.Mk.IIs without radar, and later went on to use the more effective FB.Mk.VI. Operations ranged all over Europe by day and night, attacking aircraft in the air and on the ground, as well as many other targets of opportunity. The F.Mk.IIs were only provided with the standard gun armament of four 0.303inch machine guns in the nose and four 20mm cannons under the cockpit floor, which were sufficiently destructive for the task.

Intruder operations started with No.23 Squadron under the command of Squadron Leader Sam Hoare in July 1942, with the CO claiming a Do217 only two nights after becoming operational. Moving from Ford to Manston and then Bradwell Bay to be closer to enemy targets, the score continued to grow, until with the poorer winter weather, ground targets such as trains and power installations were attacked. Following the fitting of long range fuel tanks behind the fuselage mounted cameras, giving a further 1 ½ hours endurance, No.23 Squadron moved to Malta at the end of the year.

However, the successes of No.23 Squadron had not gone unnoticed and six aircraft were selected from each of five night fighter squadrons, Nos.25, 85, 151, 157 and 284. These aircraft were modified with long-range fuel tanks, equipped with "Gee" navigation equipment, the cannon ammunition capacity was increased from 175 to 255 rounds and the bulky AI radar was removed. The night

fighter crews needed further training for intruder operations and in October 1942 a squadron from No.51 OTU at Cranfield was transferred to Twinwood Farm under the command of Sam Hoare to provide the specialist training. With the rapidly increasing growth of intruder operations, No.60 OTU was formed at High Ercall in May 1943 from the Twinwood Farm unit, to be responsible for all training in this role. With a gradual expansion, 60 OTU was eventually allocated up to fifty Mosquitos.

Deep penetrations over enemy territory on a freelance basis, attacking targets of opportunity were known as *Rangers*, and started in February 1943. Aircraft took off at pre-planned times and once airborne remained out of contact with their base. The aim was to destroy enemy aircraft in the air and on the ground, disorganise the training and attack communications, while keeping the enemy fighters at a high rate of readiness day and night. Intruders, however, were directed at pre-planned targets and remained in contact with their base. Mosquitos were also introduced to *Instep* patrols, protecting Coastal Command aircraft from enemy fighters over the Bay of Biscay. The first night *Ranger* missions were flown by Nos.25 and 151 Squadrons in mid February 1943, joined by Nos.157 and 456 Squadrons at the end of March. Also in March No.605 Squadron was equipped with Mosquitos committed to full time Intruder operations, soon to be joined by No.418 (City

Above: **A Mosquito FB.VI ready for departure on another night intruder sortie on 19 December 1944.**

Right: **Flying Officer Coates and Flight Lieutenant Sandeman watch as intruder Mosquitos depart in support of the Allied ground forces in Normandy following the D-Day landings.**

Right: **Flying Officer Coates and Flight Lieutenant Sandeman watch as intruder Mosquitos depart in support of the Allied ground forces in Normandy following the D-Day landings.**

Below: **An Intruder Mosquito FB.VI ready for departure and awaiting removal of the chocks before providing air support for the advancing troops.**

of Edmonton) Squadron RCAF. With the replacement of the F.Mk.IIs by FB.Mk.VIs the units gained the capability of carrying four 500lb (227kg) bombs and the provision of underwing drop fuel tanks brought most of Europe within range. In July 1943 Nos.418, 456 and 605 Squadrons received FB.VIs for Intruder duties and with the support of other units, continued to fly *Ranger* and bomber support duties until the end of the war. Railway installations and airfield strikes continued to be the main targets.

Day Intruder operations were hazardous due to low level flying with aircraft operating in pairs, and it was not unusual for at least one aircraft to fail to return. In contrast crews on night Intruders could complete a tour of thirty-five sorties without seeing a single target.

The navigator was tasked with map reading over Europe at night by the light of a subdued cycle lamp, while helping the pilot keep a look-out for enemy aircraft. One of these navigators was Reg Fidler who unfortunately suffered from air-sickness on most flights. Such was his keenness to

Above: **Wing Commander Sam Hoare DSO*, DFC* CO of No.605 Squadron celebrating at the Dorchester Hotel in London on 15 April, the 100th Intruder victory achieved on 10 – 11 January 1944. On the left is his navigator, Flying Officer Potter DFC, centre is Group Captain Cecil Wright AFC MP, founder of the Auxiliary Squadron. On the right is Air Commodore Sir Lindsay Everard MP, Honorary Air Commodore of the squadron.**

Left: **Flight Lieutenant Bodington and Flight Sergeant Wicks check target details before taking off on a daylight Intruder sortie in a Mosquito FB.VI in January 1944.**

fly that he just added this to his other regular airborne activities. Reg shared his flying with Henry Morley and the aircraft was fitted with *Gee* to help with navigation, but was usually flying too low for it to be effective except as a welcome homing aid on return to base. When Reg Fidler and Henry Morley were asked if they ever hit chimneys or telegraph poles, their reply was that they never flew that high.

In September 1943 the top scoring unit was No.605 Squadron, with claims for ten aircraft destroyed and two damaged. At the end of this successful month Wing Commander Sam Hoare was appointed CO of No.605 and

celebrated by destroying a Do217 on his next patrol. Sam Hoare claimed the 100th victory by No.605 Squadron on 10-11 January 1944 when he shot down a Ju188. When he left the squadron on 17 April his personal score was thirty-three shot down, two probables and a further thirty-five damaged on the ground, many beyond repair.

Henry and Reg were with No.515 Squadron based at Little Snoring, where Sam Hoare was the station commander. They claimed one confirmed night success, but their most memorable operation was the search for a colleague who had bailed out over the North Sea. The pilot had been picked up very quickly, but there was no sign of

Left: **A 500lb bomb being hoisted under the port wing of a Mosquito FB.VI by armourers.**

Above: **No.515 Squadron Mosquito FB.VIs lined up at Little Snoring in 1945.**

the navigator. Although it was August the sea was very rough and the initial search had been completed. Henry and Reg were allocated a search area, which drew a blank, but working on a hunch they went off at a tangent and were delighted to locate the missing crewman where Sunderlands, Walruses and boats had failed. A Walrus landed alongside the survivor, by which time he had drifted close to the hostile Dutch coast. After four attempts the Walrus managed to stagger into the air under the protection of the Mosquitos, while the coastal guns remained silent.

Intruder operations continued with No.515 Squadron and on 20 September 1944 two Mosquito FB.VIs , PZ440 and NS993 were allocated Holzkirchen airfield, south-east of Munich as the target. Henry and Reg were the crew of PZ440 and while pressing home their low level attacks, they were damaged by target explosions as they flew over. The fuel tanks were punctured and one engine stopped, while the other aircraft was less seriously damaged. Both aircraft set course for the safety of neutral Switzerland, but they received an unfriendly reception as PZ440 was fired at by Swiss anti-aircraft guns and attacked by fighters. As a result the other engine stopped, giving no alternative but to force land. Luckily they were not over the mountains and came in on a farm, skidding to a halt in a convenient field. The aircraft broke up around the crew, throwing out Reg who was injured, while Henry was still strapped in the cockpit. Henry clambered out of the wreckage, dragging

Below: **Mosquito NF.II HR241 with the early AI radar antenna in the nose returns from a night Intruder sortie in November 1944.**

Right: **A remarkable series of photographs showing Reg Fiddler and Henry Morley's No.515 Squadron Mosquito.** On 20 September 1944 they were tasked to attack an airfield near Munich when an engine was damaged over the target. On arrival into neutral Swiss airspace, the other engine was stopped by anti-aircraft guns, making a forced landing unavoidable. The aircraft broke-up on landing, injuring Reg, who can be seen to the right of the discarded propeller being administered a morphine injection by Henry. Meanwhile, a group of curious Swiss people are standing by the wreckage, taking no notice of the plight of the crew.

Reg clear, and gave him a morphine injection. The aircraft was written-off, but did not burn, and the two men were interned. They later returned to Britain, but did not fly on operations again. The other Mosquito had also lost an engine and made a successful forced landing, joining the increasing stock of Allied aircraft to arrive in Switzerland.

Right: **The wreckage of Mosquito FB.VI PZ440.** Henry Morley was lucky to find a level piece of ground to make his forced landing in Switzerland. Although Henry was unhurt, his navigator Reg Fiddler was injured as the cockpit structure broke-up.

SQUADRON

Code Letters:

DH*

Usage:
Mosquito FB.IV
Nov 1944 – 1945

Bases:

Benson 2.44 – 3.45
Coulommiers 3.45 – 11.45

*DH codes used post-war only.

Above: **Mosquito FB.VIs were used by No.540 Squadron for armed reconnaissance to compliment the regular unarmed PR versions.** With one engine out the Mosquito could bring its crew home safely, but the approach and landing had to be made with care as an overshoot could be difficult. The squadron's main role was in photo reconnaissance equipped with Mosquito IVs, IXs, XVIs and later PR.34s, and was the first squadron to obtain pictures of the V.1s at Peenemunde in November 1943. Mosquito FB.VIs were used by the squadron for armed reconnaissance over Scandinavia and northern Germany from late 1944 until the end of the war.

Below: **No.600 Squadron operated Mosquito NF.XIXs, similar to MM652 shown, for the night defence of Italy from December 1944.** The squadron gave support to the advancing ground forces in Italy, replacing Beaufighters with Mosquito NF.XIXs at the end of 1944. Crews were detached to the south of Italy to train on the new type, but night combats were few and far between with a final victory claimed in April. With hostilities over the squadron disbanded on 21 August 1945.

600

City of London (RAuxAF) SQUADRON

Usage:
Mosquito NF.XIX
Dec 1944 – Aug 1945

Bases:

Cesentico, Italy 12.44 – 5.45
Campoformido 5.45 – 8.45

604

County of Middlesex (RAuxAF) SQUADRON

Code Letters:

NG

Usage:
Mosquito NF.XIII
Feb 1944 – Apr 1945

Bases:

Scorton 4.43 – 4.44
Church Fenton 4.44 – 5.44
Hurn 5.44 – 7.44
Colerne 7.44
Zeals 7.44 – 8.44
France 8.44 – 9.44
Predannack 9.44 – 12.44
Odiham 12.44
Lille 12.44 – 4.45

Above: **Mosquito NF.XIII of No.604 Squadron takes off from Hurn, 1944, in support of D-Day. Typhoons of No.183 Squadron are dispersed in the background.**

Below: **The crew, Flying Officer D Gosling DFC (navigator) and Flight Lieutenant G A Hayhurst (pilot) prepare to board Mosquito NF.XIII MM617 of No.604 Squadron at Lille in January 1945.**

Service history: In February 1944 the squadron replaced its Beaufighters with Mosquitos on night defence duties. After training the squadron moved south to join the 2nd TAF on night defence of the Allied invasion forces, maintaining cover over the beaches and claiming 15 successes in the first few weeks. It was the first night fighter squadron to land in France on 6 August at Picauville with 100 victories claimed. A move was made to the more suitable airfield at Carpiquet where night patrols continued over the advancing ground forces. A return was made to Britain at the end of September until it went back to Lille on 31 December 1944. The squadron became non-operational on 15 April 1945 and disbanded at Lille three days later.

605

County of Warwick

(RAuxAF)

SQUADRON

Code Letters:

UP

Usage:
Mosquito NF.II
Feb 1943 – July 1943
Mosquito FB.VI
July 1943 – Aug 1945
Mosquito NF.30
1947 – July 1948

Bases:

Castle Camps 3.43 – 10.43
Bradwell Bay 10.43 – 4.44
Manston 4.44 – 11.44
Blackbushe 11.44 – 3.45
Coxyde, Belgium 3.45 – 4.45
Volkel, Holland 4.45 – 8.45
Honiley 6.46 - 1957

Above: **A formation of four Mosquito F.Mk.IIs from No.605 (County of Warwick) Squadron, consisting of DZ716:UP-L, DZ717, DZ724:UP-S and DZ691.**

Service history: In the intruder role, the squadron replaced a mix of Bostons and Havocs with Mosquito NF.IIs from February 1943, sometimes carrying bombs with FB.VIs. It also was involved in early night bomber support operations and celebrated the 100th confirmed enemy aircraft on 15 April 1944. With the Allied invasion in June the squadron claimed the first success over the beachhead, but they were soon deployed on anti-diver patrols. The squadron transferred from Fighter Command to the 2nd TAF at Blackbushe in September, taking on the role of close-support bombing, subsequently moving to bases in Belgium and Holland. The squadron was disbanded at Volkel on 31 August 1945 by renumbering it No.4 Squadron. No.605 Squadron was reformed in the RAuxAF in June 1946 based at Honiley with the intention of operating Mosquito NF.30s, but only received T.IIIs. In July 1948 the squadron was the first in the RAuxAF to convert to Vampires.

Below: **Flying Officer Wood (left) was navigator of a Mosquito F.Mk.II of No.605 Squadron which destroyed three enemy aircraft and four trains in one night, for which he was awarded the DFC.**

Below: **Mosquito crews of No.605 Squadron prepare for a night Intruder operation on 20 May 1943 at Castle Camps.**

608

North Riding
(RAuxAF)
SQUADRON
Code Letters:
RAO

Usage:
Mosquito NF.30
1947 – Aug 1948

Bases:

*Middleton St George
1947 – 1957*

Left: **No.608 Squadron was reformed at Thornaby in July 1946 in the light bomber role, but changed to the night fighter role with NF.30s in 1947. However, after the first summer camp at Manston in August 1948 it transferred to the day fighter role with Spitfire F.22s.**

Right: **No.609 Squadron reformed in May 1946 in the night fighter role with NF.30s and was sufficiently operational to attend a summer camp at Tangmere in 1947, but in April 1948 it became a day fighter squadron with Spitfires.**

609

West Riding
(RAuxAF)
SQUADRON
Code Letters:
RAP

Usage:
Mosquito NF.30
July 1946 – Apr 1948

Bases:

Yeadon 7.46 – 1957

613

City of Manchester
(RAuxAF)
SQUADRON

Code Letters:
SY

Usage:
Mosquito FB.VI
Oct 1943 – Aug 1945

Bases:

Lasham 10.43 – 10.44
Blackbushe 10.44 – 11.44
Cambrai, France 11.44 – 8.45

Service history: In late 1943 the squadron became part of the 2nd TAF in the light bomber role, mainly at night, and converted to Mosquito FB.VIs. In addition to the night time raids, the squadron also played a part in day precision attacks, the most notable being on 11 April 1944 against the *Gestapo* archives in the Hague, led by Wing Commander R N Bateson. Another precision raid led this time by AVM Basil Embry, AOC 2 Group, was on 18 August 1944 against a Nazi SS barracks at Egletons. On this raid fourteen Mosquitos scored at least twenty direct hits and the target was destroyed.

Above: **Mosquito FB.VI SY-W of No.613 Squadron having its oxygen bottles recharged and machine guns re-armed. This aircraft has invasion stripes painted under the rear fuselage to assist in identification over the Allied beachhead in June 1944**

Below: **Mosquito FB.VI LR366 SY-L of No.613 Squadron on operational turn around at Lasham in the Spring of 1944. This aircraft passed to No.107 Squadron on 27 July 1944 and was lost on 17 September 1944 while attacking barracks at Arnhem.**

Above: **The crew board Mosquito FB.VI LR297 of No.613 Squadron at Lasham in January 1944.**

Below: **The pilot signs for his aircraft, 'G' of No.613 Squadron at Lasham prior to another sortie over occupied Europe. (Flight photo)**

Below: **Low level precision attack by Mosquito FB.VIs of No.613 Squadron on the Hague _Gestapo_ Central Registry building on 11 April 1944.**

616

South Yorkshire

(RAuxAF)

SQUADRON

Code Letters:

RAW

Usage:
Mosquito NF.30
Nov 1946 – Dec 1948

Bases:

Finningley 7.46 – 2.57

Above: **Mosquito NF.30 NT508 RAW-E of No.616 Squadron (RAuxAF) at Finningley 1947/48.**

Right: **In a crash after an engine failure on 12 June 1945, Mosquito FB.VI HR609 of No.618 Squadron absorbed much of the shock, the cockpit remaining intact allowing the crew to escape. Even though it was made from wood, the Mosquito rarely burnt after an accident.**

618

SQUADRON

Usage:
Mosquito FB.VI
Feb 1944 – Sept 1944
Mosquito FB.XVIII
Mar 1944 – Oct 1944

Bases:

Skitten 4.43 – 9.43
Benson 9.43 – 6.44
Wick 6.44 – 10.44

683

SQUADRON

Usage:
Mosquito FB.VI
May 1943 - June 1943

Bases:

Luqa, Malta 2.43 – 11.43

684

SQUADRON

Usage:
Mosquito NF.II & FB.VI
Sept 1943 – Dec 1943

Bases:

Dum Dum, India 9.43 - 12.43

Service history: No.618 Squadron was formed at Skitten on 1 April 1943 with Mosquito B.IVs for trials with Highball bouncing bombs to be used against shipping. From December 1943 the aircrews were attached to 248 Squadron for anti U-boat operations over the Bay of Biscay. In July 1944 the squadron was re-constituted for mine laying in the Pacific, known as *Operation Oxtail*. The squadron sailed for Australia with modified Mosquito B.IVs, capable of carrying Highball weapons but never went into combat. They eventually disbanded on 25 June 1945. The aircraft were then scrapped.

TRAINING AND CONVERSION UNITS

Above: **Mosquito FB.VI, NS893**

For established operational squadrons the conversion from an earlier type of aircraft to the Mosquito was handled by the squadron. Either they were pulled out of the front line to a quieter airfield to concentrate on the task of retraining or, in a number of cases, operations continued with the old type while the Mosquito was being gradually introduced alongside and flying as a dual type squadron during the process. Meanwhile, the Operational Training Units (OTUs) were responsible for training new crews on the type and shared operational role training with the Operational Conversion Units (OCUs).

Below: **Mosquito FB.VIs of 6 OTU lined up at Kinloss in 1946.**

6 (Coastal) OTU
Code letters K7
Operated Mosquito T.III & FB.VI
Training bases:
Silloth 3.43 – 7.45,
Kinloss 7.45 – 7.47.
Service history: Reformed at Thornaby on 19 July 1941 as a coastal operational training unit, 6 OTU was mainly equipped with Wellington bombers. A move was made to Silloth on 10 March 1943 and Mosquitos arrived shortly before a move to Kinloss on 18 July 1945. The unit was renumbered 236 OCU on 31 July 1947 with Mosquito TT.35s providing support.

Above: **Mosquitos of 1655MTU, part of 16 OTU at Upper Heyford.**

Above: **Mosquito FB.VI TA503 LX of No.54 OTU with Hoverfly helicopter in the background. (DHAHC collection)**

Below: **Mosquito FB.VI NT206 9Y-AX of No.132 OTU at East Fortune.**

13 OTU
Code letters KQ, SL, XJ, FV
Operated Mosquito T.III, F.II & FB.VI
Training bases Bicester 4.40 – 10.44, Harwell 10.44 – 7.45, Middleton St George 7.45 – 4.47, Leeming 4.47 – 5.47.
Service history: The OTU was formed on 8 April 1940 initially for the training of Blenheim crews. Mosquito training was introduced on 1 November 1943 and the Blenheims had left by April 1944. With the move to Harwell, the Mosquito intermediate flight was based at the Finmere satellite from October 1944 to July 1945, and the advanced flight was based at the Hampstead Norris satellite from March to July 1945. By April 1945 the establishment included ten Mosquito T.IIIs and 55 Mosquito II/VIs. In March 1945 60 OTU was absorbed and 13 OTU was merged with 54 OTU to become 228 OCU on 1 May 1947.

16 OTU
Code letters GA, JS
Operated Mosquito T.III, FB.VI as well as bomber versions
Training bases Upper Heyford 1.45 – 3.46, Cottesmore 3.46 – 3.47
Service history: Reformed on 1 January 1945 from 1655 (Mosquito) Training Unit for mainly bomber crews, but including fighter bombers, it was disbanded on 15 March 1947 to establish 231 OCU and 204 AFS.

51 OTU
Operated Mosquito NF.II, T.III, FB.VI, NF.XII, NF.XIII, NF.XVII, NF.XIX & NF.30
Training bases Cranfield 8.41 –6.45
Service history: Initially formed at Debden on 26 July 1941 to train Blenheim night fighter crews, a move was made to 51 OTU's permanent base at Cranfield on 17 August 1941. In May 1943 Mosquito intruder training was briefly introduced, but transferred to 60 OTU, with 51 OTU concentrating on Beaufighter training. From June 1944 Mosquitos began to replace Beaufighters and the strength in December 1944 included 29 Mk.IIs, seven T.III and two FB.VI. The unit was disbanded on 14 June 1945.

54 OTU
Code letters YX, LX
Operated Mosquito NF.II, T.III, FB.VI, NF.XII, NF.XIII, NF.XVII, NF.XIX & NF.30
Training bases Charterhall 5.42 – 11.45, East Moor 11.45 – 6.46, Leeming 6.46 –5.47
Service history: Initially formed at Church Fenton on 25 November 1940 to train night fighter crews, the first Mosquito night fighters arrived at Charterhall in May 1944. By February 1945 the compliment of Mosquitos was 13 T.IIIs, 45 NF.II,FB.VI and NF.XIIs and 20 NF.XVIIs. On 1 May 1947, 54 OTU merged with 13 OTU to form 228 OCU.

60 OTU
Code letters AT
Operated Mosquito NF.II, T.III, FB.VI & B.XVI
Training bases High Ercall 5.43 – 3.45, Finmere 3 – 4.45
Service history: Reformed at High Ercall 17 May 1943 from 2 Squadron 51 OTU with Mosquitos to train crews for intruder units. In July 1943 the strength included 34 Mosquitos, which by February 1944 had grown to 17 F.IIs, 11 T.IIIs and 14 FB.VIs. 60 OTU was disbanded into 13 OTU on 11 April 1945.

132 (Coastal) OTU
Code letters 9Y
Operated Mosquito NF.II, T.III & FB.VI
Training bases East Fortune 11.42 – 5.46
Service history: Formed at East Fortune on 24 November 1942 with the role of training long range fighter and strike crews for Coastal Command initially using Blenheims and Beaufighters. Mosquitos were introduced in April 1944. On 11 February 1945, the Mosquito element moved to 8 OTU at Haverfordwest with 8 OTU, but returned to East Fortune by 17 June and the unit disbanded on 15 May 1946.

228 OCU

Operated Mosquito T.III, FB.VI, NF.30, NF.36
Training bases Leeming 5.47 – 4.46, Coltishall 1.52 – 7.52, Leeming 7.52 – 4.56, North Luffenham 4.56 – 1.57, Leeming 1.57 – 9.61
Service history: Formed on 1 May 1947 for tactical light bomber and night fighter training at Leeming by combining 13 and 54 OTUs. The initial establishment included four T.IIIs, nine FB.VIs and seven NF.30s and the two Mosquito squadrons were detached to Coltishall while the runways at Leeming were repaired. Flying was then transferred to North Luffenham in April 1956 until January 1957 while Leeming was rebuilt, and the unit disbanded on 15 September 1961.

204 AFS (Advanced Flying School)
Code letters FMO
Operated Mosquito T.III, FB.VI
Training bases Cottesmore 3.47 – 3.48, Driffield 3.48 – 8.49, Brize Norton 8.49 – 6.50, Swinderby 6.50 – 2.52, Bassingbourne 2.52
Service history: Formed 15 March 1947 at Cottesmore from a nucleus of 13 and 16 OTUs to train Mosquito crews. Became D Squadron of 231 OCU at Bassingbourn.

1672 Mosquito Training Unit

Operated Mosquito T.III, FB.VI
Training bases Yelahanka 2.44 – 6.44, Kolar 6.44 – 10.44, Yelahanka 10.44 – 8.45, Ranchi 8.45
Service history: Formed on 1 February 1944 to convert Vengeance crews to Mosquitos then being delivered to SEAC units and disbanded on 31 August 1945.

1692 Flt
Code letters 4X
Operated Mosquito NF.II, T.III, FB.VI, NF.XII, NF.XIX
Training bases Drem 7.43 – 12.43, Little Snoring 12.43 – 5.44, Great Massingham 5.44 – 6.45.
Service history: Formed around 5 July 1943 as 1692 Radio Development Flight with Defiants, Beaufighters and Mosquitos. While at Little Snoring the unit trained Mosquito crews on *Serrate* and while at Great Massingham in March 1945, the unit strength included 13 Mosquito FB.VI. It was disbanded on 16 June 1945.

9 Refresher Flying Unit

Operated Mosquito T.III, FB.VI
Training bases Ranchi, India 8.45 – 11.45
Service history: Formed 31 August 1945 from 1672 CU and disbanded on 30 November 1945.

25 APC (Armament Practice Camp)

Operated Mosquito FB.VI
Training bases Westerland, renamed Sylt 27.9.45, 7.45 – 7.46
Service history: Formed 15 July 1945 and disbanded 17 July 1946 into Training Squadron, RAF Sylt.

Armament Practice Station (APS), Acklington
Code letters 8I
Operated Mosquito T.III, FB.VI, TT.35
Training bases Acklington 5.46 – 7.56
Service history: Formed on 1 May 1946 from 2 APS at Spilsby and disbanded on 27 July 1956.

APS, Lubeck

Operated Mosquito T.III, FB.VI
Training bases Lubeck 5.46 – 9.48
Service history: Formed 1 May 1946 and disbanded on 30 September 1948

APS, Spilsby

Operated Mosquito FB.VI
Training bases Spilsby
Service history: Formed on 1 December 1945 and disbanded on 1 August 1946 to form part of APS Acklington.

Right: **Mosquito T.III RR299 FMO-B of No.204 AFS while at Driffield. This aircraft later served with 3CAACU at Exeter and after retirement to 27 MU at Shawbury it was bought by Hawker Siddeley Aviation in July 1963. The aircraft was based at Harwarden until it was lost in a fatal crash at Barton Aerodrome during an air display.**

SUPPORT UNITS

Above: **Although the Central Flying School did not operate Mosquitos in the training role, Mosquito T.III TW117:Z was flown for a short period as an historic aircraft, appearing at the Farnborough Show. Following retirement, it was preserved in the RAF Museum at Hendon, until transferred to the national aviation museum in Norway. (DHAHC collection)**

Central Bomber Establishment (CBE)
Code letters DF
Operated Mosquito T.III, FB.VI, NF.XVII + B.XVI & B.35
Bases Marham 9.45 – 4.49, Lindholme 4.49 – 12.49
Service history: Formed on 25 September 1945 at Marham and moved to Lindholme on 14 April 1949 where it disbanded on 21 December the same year.

Empire Air Armament School
Code letters FGC
Operated Mosquito FB.VI
Bases Manby 4.44 – 7.49
Service history: Formed 18 April 1944 at Manby and absorbed into the RAF Flying College (RAFFC) on 31 July 1949.

Left: **Mosquito NF.36 RL235 ZE-F of the CFE in 1946. (DHAHC collection)**

Central Fighter Establishment (CFE)
Code letters ZE
Operated Mosquito FB.VI
Bases
Wittering 10.44 – 1.45,
Tangmere 1.45 – 10.45,
West Raynham
10.45 – 10.62
Service history: Officially formed at Wittering on 1 October 1944. Moved to Tangmere on 15 January 1945 and then to West Raynham on 1 October 1945 where it remained until moving to Binbrook on 5 October 1962.

Above: **Mosquito NF.XVII ZQ-H of the Fighter Interception Unit (FIU) at Ford in October 1944.**

Below: **The aircrews of the Fighter Interception Development Unit (FIDU) at Ford in front of a Mosquito NF.XVII on 23 November 1944.**

Fighter Interception Unit (FIU)
Code letters ZQ
Operated Mosquito NF.II, FB.VI, NF.XII, NF.XIII, NF.XV, NF.XVII
Bases Tangmere 4.40 – 8.40, Shoreham 8.40 – 1.41, Ford 1.41 – 4.44, Wittering 4.44 – 8.44, Ford 8.44
Service history: Formed 18 April 1940 initially to test new night fighter equipment, but eventually the duties expanded. It was redesignated the Fighter Interception Development Unit (FIDU) on 31 August 1944.

FIDU
Code letters ZQ
Operated Mosquito NF.II, FB.VI, NF.XII, NF.XIII, NF.XVII
Bases Ford 8.44 – 7.45, Tangmere 7.45 – 10.45, West Raynham 10.45 – 7.50
Service history: Formed 31 August 1944 from FIU and became the Fighter Interception Development Squadron of the Night Fighter Development Wing, CFE when the CFE was formed on 1 October 1944. After moves to Tangmere and West Raynham it became the Radar Interception Development Squadron in July 1950.

Central Gunnery School (CGS)
Code letters FJT
Operated Mosquito FB.VI
Bases Warmwell 11.39 – 6.41, Castle Kennedy 6.41 – 12.41, Chelveston 12.41 – 4.42, Sutton Bridge 4.42 – 2.44, Catfoss 2.44 – 11.45, Leconfield 11.45 – 12.46
Service history: Formed on 6 November 1939 at Warmwell to improve the standard of RAF air gunnery and in December 1946 the strength included 13 Mosquito FB.VIs. It disbanded on 31 December 1954 to form the Fighter Weapons School and Coastal Command Gunnery School.

Empire Central Flying School (ECFS)

Operated Mosquito T.III, FB.VI + B.25 & B.35
Bases Hullavington 4.42 – 5.46
Service history: Formed on 1 April 1942 from nucleus of CFS to provide instruction techniques in numerous types of aircraft. In June 1944 the establishment included two Mosquito FB.VIs and the unit was redesignated the Empire Flying School on 7 May 1946.

Empire Flying School (EFS)
Code letters FCX
Operated Mosquito T.III, FB.VI, NF.30, NF.38
Bases Hullavington 5.46 – 7.49
Service history: Formed 7 May 1946 from ECFS and disbanded into RAF Flying College 31 July 1949.

Fighter Experimental Flight

Operated Mosquito NF.30
Bases Wittering 10.44 – 6.45
Service history: Formed on 1 October 1944 at Wittering as the Night Fighter Development Wing of the CFS. Commenced intruder operations using Coltishall as an advanced base and disbanded in June 1945.

Night Fighter Development Wing

Operated Mosquito FB.VI, NF.XIII, NF.XVII, NF.30
Bases Ford 10.44 – 7.45, Tangmere 7.45 – 10.45, West Raynham 10.45
Service history: Formed on 16 October 1944 as part of the CFE incorporating the FIU. After a move to Tangmere in July 1945, the unit was absorbed into the CFE at West Raynham on 1 October 1945.

Highball Trials Flight

Operated Mosquito FB.VI + B.IV & TR.33
Bases Spilsby 4.46 – 6.46, Coningsby 6.46 – 11.47
Service history: As a detachment of the MAEE it was sent to Spilsby on 1 April 1946 and moved to Coningsby on 1 June until 7 November 1947.

Below: **Mosquito F.IIs on the production line at Hatfield.**

Production Batches

de Havilland, Hatfield
W4052, *prototype NF.II*
W4073 *F.II*
W4075, W4077 *T.III*

W4074, W4076, W4078,
W4080, W4082, W4084,
W4086 - 4099 *NF.II*
24 out of the first 50 aircraft.

DD600 – 644
DK308 – 333
DK336 – 339
150 F.IIs

DZ228 – 272
DZ286 – 310
70 F.IIs

DZ653 – 661
DZ680 – 727
DZ739 – 761
80 F.IIs

HJ642 – 661
HJ699 – 715
37 NF.IIs

HJ662 – 682
HJ716 – 743
HJ755 – 792
HJ808 – 833
113 FB.VI

HX802 –835
HX849 – 869
HX896 – 922
HX937 – 984
130 FB.VI

LR248 – 276
LR289 – 313
LR327 – 340
LR343 – 389
LR402 – 404
118 FB.VI

MM398 – 423
MM426 – 431
32 FB.VI

MM424 – 425
2 FB.XVIII

MP469. *1 NF.XV*

NS819 – 859
NS873 – 914

NS926 – 965
NS977 – 999
NT112 – 156
NT169 – 207
NT219 – 238
(NT220, NT224,
NT225 - 3 - *FB.XVIII*)
250 FB.VI

PZ161 – 203
PZ217 – 259
PZ273 – 316
PZ330 – 358
PZ371 – 419
PZ435 – 476
(*including 9 FB.XVIII*)
250 FB.VI

RS501 – 535
RS548 – 580
RS593 – 633
109 FB.VI

SZ958 – 999
TA113 – 122
52 FB.VI

TA123 – 156
TA169 – 198
TA215 – 249
TA263 – 308
TA323 – 357
180 NF.XIX

TA369 – 388
20 FB.VI

TA389 – 413
TA425 – 449
50 NF.XIX

TA469 – 508
TA523 – 560
TA575 – 603
107 FB.VI

VP342 – 355
VR330 – 349
34 T.III

VT581 – 596
VT604 – 631
44 T.III

VT651 – 669
19 NF.38

de Havilland, Leavesden
HJ851 – 899
HJ958 – 999
91 T.III

HJ911 – 944
34 F.II

HJ945 – 946
HK107 – 141
HK159 – 204
HK222 – 235
*97 F.II (converted to NF.XII
by Marshall of Cambridge)*

HK363 – 382
HK396 – 437
HK453 – 481
HK499 – 536
129 NF.XIII

LR516 – 541
LR553 – 585
59 T.III

MM436 – 479
MM491 – 534
MM547 – 590
MM615 – 623
141 NF.XIII

MM624 – 656
MM669 – 685
50 NF.XIX

MM686 – 710
MM726 – 769
MM783 – 822
109 NF.30

MT456 – 500
MV521 – 570
95 NF.30

NT241 – 283
NT295 – 336
NT349 – 393
NT415 – 458
NT471 – 513
NT526 – 568
NT582 – 621
300 NF.30

RK929 – 954
26 NF.30

RK955 – 960
RK972 – 999
RL113 – 158
RL173 – 215
EL229 – 268

236 NF.36
RL248 *NF.38 Prototype*

RR270 – 319
50 T.III
TN954 – 984
TW101 – 119
50 T.III

VA871 – 894
VA923 – 928
30 T.III

de Havilland, Hawarden
VX860 – 879
VX886 – 916
51 NF.38 (last completed
November 1950)

Airspeed, Christchurch
RS637 – 680
RS693 – 698
50 FB.VI

VL726 – 732
7 FB.VI

**Standard Motors,
Coventry**
HP848 – 888
HP904 – 942
HP967 – 989
HR113 – 162
HR175 – 220
HR236 – 262
HR279 – 312
HR331 – 375
HR387 – 415
HR432 – 465
HR485 – 527
HR539 – 580
HR603 – 649
250 FB.VI

RF580 – 625
RF639 – 681
RF695 – 736
RF749 – 753
RF818 – 859
RF873 – 915
RF928 – 966
300 FB.VI

TE587 – 628
TE640 – 669
TE683 – 725
TE738 – 780
TE793 – 830
TE848 – 889
TE905 – 932
266 FB.VI

SQUADRON / CODES		SQUADRON / CODES		SQUADRON / CODES		OTHER UNITS	
4	UP, NC	141	TW	456	RX		
11	OM	143	NE	464	SB	6 OTU	
21	YH	151	DZ	487	EG	13 OTU	KQ,SL,XJ,FV
22		157	RS	488	ME	16 OTU	GA, JS
23	YP	169	VI	489	P6	54 OTU	YX, LX
25	ZK	176		500	RAA	60 OTU	AT
27		199		502	RAC	132 OTU	9Y
29	RO	211		504	RAD	288 OCU	
36	DM	219	FK	515	3P	204 AFS	FMO
39		235	LA	540	DH	1672	MTU
45	OB	239	HB	600		1692 Flt	4X
46		248	DM	604	NG	9 RFU	
47	KU	249	GN	605	UP	25 APC	
55		254	QM	608	RAO	APS	8I
68	WM	255	YD	609	RAP	CBE	DF
69	WI	256	JT	613	SY	CFE	ZE
82	UX	264	PS	616	RAW	CGS	FJT
84	PY	268		618		EAAS	FGC
85	VY	305	SM	683		ECFS	
89		307	EW	684		EFS	FCX
96	ZJ	333	KK			FEF	
107	OM	404	EO			FIU	ZQ
108		406	HU			FIDU	ZQ
110	VE	409	KP			NFDW	
114	RT	410	RA			HTF	
125	VA	418	TH				

Below: **Showing the Codes RX denoting No.456 Squadron is Hatfield built Mosquito NF.Mk.II DD739**

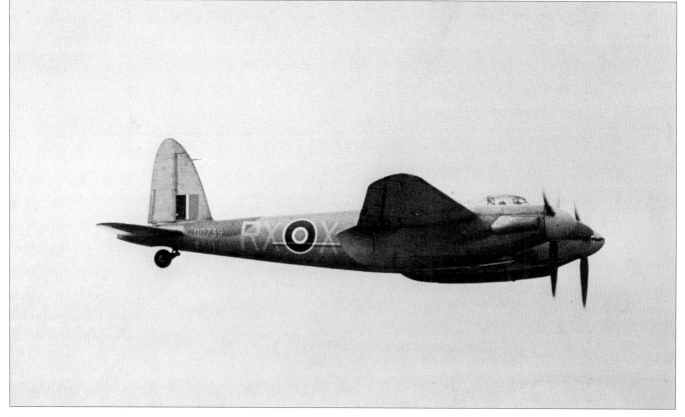